Performance and Reward Management

Florence Stone

- Fast track route to mastering performance and reward management

- Covers the key areas of performance and reward management, from conducting performance appraisals effectively and efficiently and recognizing outstanding work when money is in short supply to learning how today's companies are using reward systems to achieve corporate missions and strategies

- Examples and lessons from some of the world's most successful businesses, including Johnson & Johnson, Hewlett Packard, Royal Dutch Shell, TRW and Motorola, and ideas from the smartest thinkers, including Abraham Maslow, Frederick Herzberg, Peter Drucker, Henry Mintzberg, Tom Peters and Jac Fitz-enz

- Includes a glossary of key concepts and a comprehensive resources guide.

PEOPLE

09.09

essential management thinking at your fingertips

The right of Florence Stone to be identified as the author of this work has been asserted in accordance with the Copyright, Designs and Patents Act 1988

First published 2002 by
Capstone Publishing (a Wiley company)
8 Newtec Place
Magdalen Road
Oxford OX4 1RE
United Kingdom
http://www.capstoneideas.com

CIP catalogue records for this book are available from the British Library and the US Library of Congress

ISBN 1-84112-207-6

Substantial discounts on bulk quantities of Capstone books are available to corporations, professional associations and other organizations. Please contact Capstone for more details on +44 (0)1865 798 623 or (fax) +44 (0)1865 240 941 or (e-mail) info@wiley-capstone.co.uk

FSC
Mixed Sources
oduct group from well-managed
ests and other controlled sources

Cert no. SGS-COC-2953
www.fsc.org
© 1996 Forest Stewardship Council

Contents

Introduction to ExpressExec

ExpressExec is 3 million words of the latest management thinking compiled into 10 modules. Each module contains 10 individual titles forming a comprehensive resource of current business practice written by leading practitioners in their field. From brand management to balanced scorecard, ExpressExec enables you to grasp the key concepts behind each subject and implement the theory immediately. Each of the 100 titles is available in print and electronic formats.

Through the ExpressExec.com Website you will discover that you can access the complete resource in a number of ways:

» printed books or e-books;
» e-content – PDF or XML (for licensed syndication) adding value to an intranet or Internet site;
» a corporate e-learning/knowledge management solution providing a cost-effective platform for developing skills and sharing knowledge within an organization;
» bespoke delivery – tailored solutions to solve your need.

Why not visit www.expressexec.com and register for free key management briefings, a monthly newsletter and interactive skills checklists. Share your ideas about ExpressExec and your thoughts about business today.

Please contact elound@wiley-capstone.co.uk for more information.

Introduction

This book is about how we can most effectively and efficiently recognize and reward employees. In this introductory chapter, you will learn why this topic is hot right now. For instance, you will read how important it is to:

» link performance objectives to business goals or mission;
» monitor efforts to reach those goals; and
» assess performance annually and reward accordingly with pay for heightened performance.

When we talk about performance management, invariably the subject of performance appraisals arises. But appraisals – the annual assessments of employee job performance – are only one segment of performance management, which is a process for establishing a shared understanding about what is to be accomplished and rewarding people in a manner that increases the probability of their achieving success. That process also includes coaching, in which training and ongoing feedback are provided to sustain good performance, and counseling, in which troubled or troublesome employees are advised with the goal of turning around sub-par performance. Aligned to performance management is another process, reward management, which involves development of a compensation and benefits program that truly distinguishes outstanding performance with recognition and rewards. Which increasingly includes variable pay.

Research conducted by Edward Lawler indicates that a pay increase of 3–4%, while noticeable, is not sufficient to improve performance. The Hay Group reports that since 1996, annual merit increases have been around 4%, although a 4% increase on, say, a $50,000 salary, if taxes are around 30%, is a new paycheck only $27 higher than the old paycheck.

In this book, you will learn how to:

» link performance objectives to specific business goals or mission and communicate these clearly to employees;
» monitor efforts to reach those goals, including job behaviors, providing ongoing feedback;
» complete formal assessments of each employee's performance at least once a year following corporate policies and procedures. Opponents of performance appraisals point to the difficulty of setting measurable goals and the problems with appraisals in measuring the wrong aspects of performance and creating conflicts among employees, but studies of companies with appraisal programs show that they outperform companies without such programs on a wide range of financial and productivity measures; and
» take a total approach to rewards, integrating the rewards into how employees are managed. To do this, you will need to understand better the various rewards available – extrinsic and intrinsic – and how each is presumed to work. This book will identify current pay

and benefit programs, their impact in good and bad economic times, and innovative reward systems for the changing workplace.

Why this emphasis on performance management systems and performance-based rewards? Solid management of employee performance is critical in today's competitive, global marketplace. Organizations don't act – people do. Your responsibility as a manager is to ensure that your employees complete effectively and efficiently those tasks critical to the organization's business goals. When you fail to do this, you fail to fulfill your own responsibilities as a manager and as their supervisor. The human resources division creates both a performance management system and a reward management system that are designed to drive strategy and business goals. They work to avoid the frequent criticism given of both: lenient ratings, sugar-coated feedback, ambiguous standards that don't reflect the need for greater productivity and profitability, and pay-for-performance plans that don't provide incentive for increased performance. But it is only their organization's managers who can make the performance and reward management systems a success.

Definition of Terms

In this chapter you will learn about:

- » SMART goals;
- » documentation;
- » intrinsic and extrinsic rewards, monetary and non-monetary rewards; and
- » performance and reward systems.

If you are to fully appreciate the benefits of effective, efficient performance management and reward management, you need to have a clear idea of the terminology. This chapter will look at the meanings of:

» performance management;
» reward management; and
» related terms.

Performance management is, obviously, a process but it is one built around a proactive partnership between employees and managers that helps employees perform at their best and align their contribution with the goals, values, and initiatives of the organization.

The phrase "proactive partnership" is particularly suitable, since a critical part of performance management is creation of an agreement – a "performance management contract" – between a supervisor and each of his or her employees in which both agree to a set of standards, goals, or results for which the employee will be held accountable during a specific period of time, usually a year, with milestones or periodic reviews to discuss progress.

Reward management is also a process, one designed to encourage continual outstanding performance. Employees receive a base pay or salary based on the importance of their position, value placed on their skills in the marketplace, and experience of the job holders, plus variable pay that is a measure of the quality of their performance. That variable pay is given only when performance justifies it, and it can take the form of a "bonus" or one-time reward for outstanding output. There are various terms for the last, including gain sharing, win sharing, and profit sharing. The use of "merit increases" is declining. Employees see little motivation in increases of 3–4%, the usual percentage of merit increase that over time has come to be seen as an "entitlement," a given for remaining with the company with little concern for the quality or quantity of performance.

Goals specified in the performance contract or other form used by the organization are tied to the broader goals of the department or division or, even broader, the goals of the organization as a whole. Aligning the direction of individual departments and employees within those departments is essential to implement a successful performance management system. When everyone speaks the same language, and goals are in alignment, employees are more focused and have a clear understanding of how they can contribute to the bigger picture.

As the goals are written, they should meet five criteria. To remember these, management experts use the acronym SMART.

» *S for Specific*. Vague goals mean little. What do I mean by "vague"? "Improve customer satisfaction" or "reduce errors." They may be movements in the right direction but they are impossible to measure or quantify. In order to make goals specific, a manager has to define how they will be measured. Which brings us to. . .

» *M for Measurable*. The manager should be able to measure results to determine if his or her employee is meeting the goal. For instance, let's take the earlier goal, "improve customer satisfaction." A goal that is both specific and measurable would be "achieve an average customer satisfaction rating of 90% by the end of the year." So would "cut paperwork errors by 5% by the end of the first quarter."

Ideally, as the goals are being written, the manager should look for ways to break longer-term goals down into bite-sized, more manageable goals by setting targets for review during the quarterly or trimester milestone evaluations.

» *A is for Accountable*. Accountability really has two meanings. First, and foremost, goals should be accountable in that the employee has the authority to achieve the goal – and all within the organization know so. Second, and even more important, the individual should have accepted accountability for achieving the goals. Too often, goals are set but employees don't buy into them; that is, agree to work toward their achievement. Without this, employees aren't likely to make any effort to achieve the goals.

» *R is for Realistic*. The question is, "Can the goal be accomplished?" Goals should, yes, have "stretch"; that is, they should offer some challenge. Ideally, goals set should not be so low that they have no meaning but not so unreachable that employees become discouraged, aware that they can't achieve them.

Besides the goals themselves being realistic, the number of goals, too, should be realistic. That is, it is better to have five SMART goals that can be reached than 10 goals that will never get accomplished.

» *T is for Time-related*. When you write down a goal, you should specify when the goal will be accomplished. An open-ended goal without a specific date is likely never to be achieved or, at the very least, to be put at the bottom of a priority list.

As managers undertake performance management, many ask the question: Why? After all, the process is time-consuming. Not only the one-on-one meetings with employees during which goals are set but also the follow-up progress sessions and end-of-year appraisal interview during which the employee's work over the 12-month period is assessed based on documentation, like information contained in "critical incident reports" or appraisal journals. Let's look at the benefits of performance management and well-managed reward systems.

» *Improved performance*: When performance is managed, it tends to be better. Why? Employees work harder when they know their manager is interested in them and what they are doing.
» *Improved communication*: A proactive partnership with employees requires ongoing communication, critical to effective performance.
» *Organization alignment*: When individual goals relate to organizational objectives, there is alignment up and down the line, thereby increasing the odds of achievement of organization objectives. People and/or departments aren't working at cross-purposes. Employees are focused on the same major priorities and all have a clear understanding of how they can support the organization's overall success.
» *Organization capability*: More can be accomplished by the firm as a whole when everyone within the organization is pulling in the same direction via the performance management system.
» *Increased employee self-management*: Employees know their manager's expectations and are in a position to take responsibility themselves for their work hours. For one, they can set priorities for themselves rather than depend on their manager to do so. They know what tasks are most critical.
» *Increased employee satisfaction*: Employees like to have clear expectations and get feedback about how well they are doing. That's what the performance management system does. Also, the more responsible employees are in planning and carrying out their goals, the more satisfaction they will have in their jobs.

Like most processes, performance management only works when the process is followed carefully. There are six steps.

1 *Communicate expectations*: Other words for expectations are "standards," "goals," or "results." When employees know what is expected, they will rise not only to meet those expectations but even to exceed them. A major cause of poor or substandard performance is that people don't know what is expected. When they don't know what the goals are, they won't know when or if they have hit them.

   Expectations play a critical part in every step in the performance management process. For instance, when setting goals, both employee and manager must have a clear idea about what is to be accomplished, by when, and if there are any budgetary constraints. When monitoring performance, there has to be agreement on what will be monitored. Disagreements occur when the employee expects one thing to be monitored and the manager looks at something else. Finally, if performance problems occur, expectations for improvement need to be clearly communicated. Likewise, the consequences of failure to improve performance, like termination.

2 *Involve employees in the process*: As mentioned, performance management is a partnership. Managers and employees must work together. If they see themselves as adversaries, then neither the manager nor the employee will benefit. There is an acronym WIIFM – *what's in it for me*. Both the manager's and employee's commitment to performance management will depend on the WIIFM. For the employee, the WIIFM may be the opportunity for financial reward or promotion (extrinsic rewards or rewards that come from the organization) or pride in a job well regarded or in overcoming a challenging problem (intrinsic rewards that come from within). For the manager, the WIIFM is work completed as needed to achieve the department's goals (*which will make the manager look good*).

3 *Use a systematic process*: I've mentioned that performance management is a process. It's important to keep this in mind – performance management is a related series of activities that when done with each and every employee contributes to the organization as a whole. Each step is designed to move the organization closer and closer to

its final business goals. By itself, each step may have minimal impact. However, when all the steps are followed, and employees accomplish their goals as a consequence, then the outcome is not only continual job performance but accomplishment of the corporate objectives.

4 *Accept the time commitment*: Yes, effective performance management takes time in the beginning – in particular, to transform general thoughts and ideas into SMART goals and to determine how to monitor and analyze how the goals are being achieved. Further, it takes additional commitment of time and effort to meet regularly with employees to review progress toward achievement of the goals – at least three to four times a year with each and every employee.

5 *Make a commitment to success*: It's very easy to begin with great fervor only to let enthusiasm wane as the year passes. Sometimes, managers blame it on the excessive forms that many performance management systems demand be completed. Other times, they argue that their own work day gives them little time to meet with their employees to conduct quarterly reviews. Whatever the excuse, at the end of the year, the dialogue that the performance management system is designed to trigger fails to lead to the honest exchange between supervisor and employee that ultimately should encourage improved performance.

Having an effective discussion about performance over the year is the real key to using performance appraisals within performance management systems. It's not in the paperwork that human resources demands. It's not even in the end-of-the-year assessment in which the manager shares his or her conclusions. Rather, it is in the ongoing communications about performance based on the goals set at the beginning of the year.

Where does the issue of rewards come in? Pay for performance – whether in the form of a bonus or more traditional merit increase – is a goal, not an entitlement. The goal of human resources is to keep as much of a link between pay and organizational strategy as possible. The manager's role is to ensure, to the best of his or her ability, that people are rewarded in accordance with their work – both monetary and non-monetary.

One last point: Non-monetary rewards (like attendance at a seminar or a high-visibility assignment, or time off to run a personal errand) have to be as earned as pay. Which means that non-monetary rewards should also be for work in alignment with the company's direction.

Evolution

This chapter covers how the behavioralists have contributed to today's performance management and reward systems. As important, discover how more recently:

» plans are under way at some companies to abolish performance appraisals;
» variable pay is making up a major part of pay-for-performance plans;
» performance systems are being linked to development efforts; and
» training is being regarded as a benefit.

Only a few organizations and the military used formal performance appraisals prior to World War II. Those programs also focused more on an individual's personality and traits than on actual achievements against goals or behaviors that produced those results. Influenced by Peter Drucker's concept of Management by Objectives (MBO), companies moved from trait assessment to implementation of a process that concentrated on goal setting, placed responsibility with the employer for achieving those goals with the employee, and made the appraisal procedure a shared responsibility between the employee and his or her manager.

Early practices of this in companies by General Electric and General Mills were used by behaviorist Douglas McGregor in his book *The Human Side of Enterprise*[1] as models for his analysis of the appraisal process.

In his book, McGregor identified three needs that formal performance appraisals were designed to meet:

1 provide systematic judgments to back up salary increases, promotions, and sometimes demotions and terminations;
2 tell an employee how he or she is doing and, better, suggest needed changes in behavior, attitudes, skills, or job knowledge; and
3 offer direction for coaching and counseling to improve performance.

Much of the early thinking about performance management and reward systems can be traced to the work of the motivational behaviorists, researchers like Abraham Maslow, Frederick Herzberg, David C. McClelland, George Elton Mayo, and finally Douglas McGregor.

Maslow hypothesized a pyramidical hierarchy of needs. At the lowest level are physiological needs – needs for food, drink, and shelter. The next level of need is safety, which included needs for security, stability, and freedom from fear. The third level of needs – social needs – involves friendships and contacts with others. Esteem and self-actualization are at the highest level of the pyramid. Esteem needs are met when we feel important or are needed by others, and self-actualization needs are fulfilled when we realize our full potential. It was over 40 years ago, and at the time about 85% of employees surveyed were satisfied in their physiological needs, 70% in their safety needs, 50% in their social needs, 40% in their ego needs, and only 10%

in their self-actualizing needs. A significant improvement in employee performance would come, Maslow believed, from giving employees the opportunity to realize more of their potential on the job.

As described in his Two-Factor Theory, Herzberg's conclusions were very similar to those of Maslow. Herzberg divided people's needs into five dissatisfiers and five satisfiers. The five satisfiers included achievement, recognition, interesting responsibilities, positive work relationships, and opportunity for growth. The five dissatisfiers were supervision (a manager willing to teach and delegate responsibility), administration (including good communication with the employee), working conditions, interrelationships, and salary (adequate compensation). Herzberg contended that a good hygienic environment could prevent job dissatisfaction but couldn't affect satisfaction. Only the job satisfiers could do that.

McClelland identified the needs of self-motivated achievers, who he believed made up about 10% of the population. These achievers preferred to set their own goals, set goals that were tough but realistic, and preferred tasks that provided them with immediate feedback. He felt it was possible to build achievement traits into jobs by including personal responsibility, individual participation in setting productivity targets, creation of moderate goals, and fast, clear-cut feedback on results.

Mayo argued in favor of small work groups in motivating workers. He felt that when people become part of an informal work group, they experience a social relationship that increases their experience. His research was supported by the experiences of Japanese companies in using teams. US company experiences with teams in the 1980s and early 1990s stimulated the love affair with teams.

What about McGregor? He conceived of Theory X and Theory Y. Theory X managers assume that all employees lack a work ethic unless proven otherwise, whereas his more participative Theory Y managers think most people have a strong work ethic and just need the opportunity to prove it. Conscientious, industrious, committed to work, and motivated – all are adjectives that are used to describe those who possess the work ethic.

So the research community set the platform for thinking about performance management and triggers to stimulate performance.

On a more practical level, test of a formal MBO-type appraisal program at General Electric, as reported by Meyer *et al.*,[2] found that the idea of performance appraisal was a good one yet few operating managers would initiate the program. The study showed that most managers carry out performance appraisal interviews only when strong control procedures were established to ensure they did them. The study did find that performance did improve when specific, mutually agreed upon goals were established. On the other hand, the researchers also said that coaching demanded day-to-day follow-up – once-a-year reviews were insufficient.

Further, the researchers found that praise had little worth in improving job performance, nor did criticism.

In essence, the study raised serious doubts about annual reviews, doubts that continue to exist today.

For instance, in observing the current state of affairs in performance appraisals in the early 1990s, writer Ron Zemke, in an article entitled "Do Performance Appraisals Change Performance?",[3] noted how uncomfortable managers felt in playing the role of God in assessing employees' performance. Yes, common wisdom held that appraisals were important to improving performance, he said, but "there is remarkably little evidence that this highly touted, widely used, and much researched process actually improves employee performance." Not only is there doubt about whether it will substantially help managers improve employee contribution in both the short term and the long term, but also whether it is an effective and efficient means for making judgments about compensation.

Zemke isn't the only management thinker to question it. Writing in *Training*'s May 1991 magazine,[4] David L. De Vries, former vice president of the Center for Creative Leadership, pointed out that only one study had showed the effectiveness of appraisal reviews but he believed that program's success was solely attributable to the support it was given by senior management. One of those who implemented the program was Gary Latham, professor of organizational effectiveness at the University of Toronto. Latham, with Edwin A. Locke of the University of Maryland, authored the book *Goal Setting: A Motivational Technique That Works*,[5] in which he observed that productivity can be increased significantly if supervisors set a specific production goals and provide attention and support to workers but also pointed to the shortfalls in implementation that make such efforts ineffective.

He pointed to the ineffectiveness of easy or vague goals like "do your best," to lack of feedback (although he also observed that feedback alone wouldn't improve performance), and to the lack of stretch in goals set over time by managers and employees. Feedback on goal-directed performance motivates higher performance only when it contributes to the setting of higher performance.

What about the role of compensation? A report in 1994 by the Society for Human Resource Management (SHRM) and Development Dimensions International (DDI) entitled *Performance Management: What's Hot – What's Not, A National Study of Current and Future Practices*,[6] suggested that managers and staff see performance management not only as a means to improve people's performance and help them grow but also as a mechanism for compensation and promotion. Such a combination, said the report, rarely succeeds. Respondents did not see a clear link between their performance and their pay.

Another study – by Robert Bretz and George Milkovich – pointed to the scarcity of rewards to those who take the process seriously and even noted that there were many informal rewards for not delivering unpopular feedback. Their study, reported by Steven L. Thomas and Robert Bretz,[7] pointed to a major fault in appraisals: managers are not commonly held accountable for how well they undertake performance appraisals. Despite all the positive talk about the benefits of annual reviews, the two found that not a lot of time is devoted to it – an average of eight hours per employee per year for appraising executives, six hours per year per professional, and fewer than four hours per year per nonexempt. The two researchers surveyed FORTUNE 100 firms, and while nine out of ten of the 70 who responded said they provided rated training in how to conduct appraisal interviews and provide feedback, the researchers discovered that the training almost always occurred during the initial development of the system, with little ongoing training.

Asked how the companies used the information generated by the appraisal process, Bretz and Milkovich found that improving work performance was, naturally, first, but, in order of importance, administering merit pay was second. Fifth had to do with making promotion decisions. The remaining top seven dealt with traditional performance issues, from advising employees of work expectations to counseling employees, to assessing employee potential, to identifying training needs, to creating better work relationships, to helping employees set career goals.

Because pay issues were closely tied to assessments, the two researchers delved into ratings and discovered skewed performance distributions to be a problem, and over two-thirds of the companies that responded to the survey reported that such skewing affected pay administration and the ability to reward the best performers. Examining the distribution of performance ratings, Bretz and Milkovich found that most companies used five performance levels but only the three highest levels were actually used. The authors suggested that these companies had a "leniency bias" associated with their assessments, with few employees rated in the bottom two levels.

As organizations moved in the mid-1990s to implement peer evaluations and team-based assessment and pay systems, a study published in *Psychological Bulletin* (87, 1) found that peer assessments were no tougher than those of bosses.[8] Authors Frank Landy and James Farr found that supervisors were not less lenient in their ratings than were the peers or the ratees. On the other hand, they found that supervisors were more consistent in their ratings than were peers. Peers tended to be more lenient than supervisors but they also were more accurate in predicting best talent for promotions.

Regardless of doubts raised about ratings, a study by William M. Mercer Consulting in 1995 suggested that 84 per cent of responding companies would continue to use the results of performance appraisals to affect merit raises.

As we enter the new millennium, despite the widespread dissatisfaction with almost everything concerned with performance appraisals, it is safe to say that performance appraisals will be the keystone of performance management programs. The overwhelming majority of organizations – large and small – use some version, and while there is some discussion about abolishing structured programs there is little likelihood that will occur.

Appraisals are here to stay. Pay programs have undergone changes over the last decade, and they can be expected to continue to change. The flawed approach to pay for performance is responsible for many of the changes.

In the past, companies relied on either an automatic step progression or a merit range approach to base pay. But neither rewarded improved performance. Automatic raises did not reflect the quantity or quality of job performance. Merit increases were a reflection of available funds allocated for pay increases – where budgets were tight, employees received little or nothing, regardless of the measure of their performance. Even in good economic times, merit increases have often been equal to cost of living increases, averaging 3–4%. In real dollars, this frequently has meant little in spendable funds.

In recent years, new approaches to base pay have appeared. They include the following.

» *Skill-based pay*. The assumption here is that more pay is given as more skills are acquired. The skills are those tied to specific requirements within the business, and pay is related directly to the total number of steps or skill bundles upon which an employee has shown capability. Opportunities are provided to increase skill capability and increases are given to reflect the multiple skills of employees.

» *Competency-based pay*. Like skill-based pay, competency-based pay increases as new skills, abilities, knowledge, or attitudes are exhibited, these competencies all tied to different positions and experience levels.

» *Team-based pay*. In team-based organizations, each person's pay raise is a portion of the merit increase earned by the team's accomplishments. A variation of this is to include team performance as a criteria for an individual's performance.

» *Lump-sum distribution*. The lump-sum in lieu approach is used primarily to reward employees who already are paid at a very high range and/or are at the top of their grade's pay level and consequently aren't eligible for base pay changes. Another approach with limited application is tying base pay to market rate and granting merit money annually in a lump sum, never rolling it into the base pay.

When we talk about pay today, however, we need to talk about "total pay," which is a combination of base pay, variable pay, and recognition.

The roots of variable pay can be traced as far ago as the 1800s in the textile industry. Piece rates changed depending on individual productivity. In the more recent past, where individual performance could be measured, it was reflected in pay. Fruit picking and sewing garments were natural tasks for variable pay, but today variable pay is also being used to reward physicians in a medical group who are paid based on patient access and satisfaction, quality of care, and patient load. As you can see, variable pay is no longer solely a measure of quantity of work. Variable pay is for value added to the organization from an individual's performance.

Since the mid-1990s, variable pay has become a part of total pay for all employees, from administrative assistants to their supervisors to senior executives. Recently, as the economy declined, there was concern as employers paid out bonuses to employees and managers whether they met department or organization goals or not. Just as merit increases became thought of as an entitlement, so, too, has variable pay.

As we experience tough times, we can expect tighter reins on bonus plans, goal sharing, win sharing, cash profit sharing, and team variable pay programs. Goal sharing is given when goals aligned with the operating plan are met or exceeded. Win sharing is tied to goals met but linked specifically to financial goals. Unless financial goals are met, no variable pay is given, regardless of other goals reached.

Bonuses are given for outstanding individual performance, beyond the job description.

Cash profit sharing is exactly what it seems – a percentage of profits is shared and distributed equally as a percentage to the staff regardless of base pay.

There are various options open to compensation managers. Many experts believe that the future will see the mixing and matching of variable pay as a portion of total pay. Non-monetary recognition will complete the pay package.

TIMELINE

Prior to the 1960s

» Base pay with merit increases
» Minimal use of structured performance appraisals based on results or behaviors; evaluations based on traits or personality
» Motivational thinkers study the causes of increased job performance/job satisfaction
  » the work of Abraham Maslow;
  » the work of Frederick Herzberg;
  » the work of David C. McClelland;
  » the work of Douglas McGregor;
  » the work of Peter Drucker.

1960s–1980s

» Introduction of variable pay (e.g., bonuses) into salary mix
» Performance appraisal systems built around Management by Objectives (results) and work behaviors implemented. Studies question implementation but considered it the best means of improving job performance.

1980s–2002

» Questions continue about validity of formal performance appraisal programs. Shift to goals aligned to strategic plans to support pay for performance efforts
» Expansion of variable pay plans throughout organizations in form of bonuses, profit sharing, win sharing, and gain sharing. Team-based pay plan as teams become means of accomplishing projects.

NOTES

1 McGregor, D. (1985) *The Human Side of Enterprise*. McGraw-Hill Higher Education, New York.

2 Meyer, H.H., Kay, E. & French, J.R.P., Jr. (1995) "Split Roles in Performance Appraisal." *Harvard Business Review*, Jan–Feb.

3 Zemke, R. (1991) "Do Performance Appraisals Change Performance?" *Training*, May.

4 De Vries, D.L. (1991) *Training*, May.

5 Latham, G. & Locke, E.A. (1990) *Goal Setting: A Motivational Technique That Works*. Prentice-Hall, NJ.

6 SHRM & DDI (1994) *Performance Management: What's Hot –What's Not, A National Study of Current and Future Practices*. SHRM, Chicago.

7 Thomas, S.L. & Bretz, R. (1994) "Research and Practice in Performance Appraisal: Evaluating Employee Performance in America's Largest Companies." *SAM Advanced Management Journal*, Spring.

8 Landy, F. & Farr, J. (1987) *Psychological Bulletin*, 87, 1.

The E-Dimension

This chapter gives information on:

- » how you evaluate those who telecommute;
- » software programs to facilitate assessment writing;
- » integration of payroll programs in human resource information systems; and
- » employee information that can be maintained on the company's HRIS.

Electronic technology has created a supervision problem but it has also provided a means to manage better the data related to supervision, from performance management to compensation and benefits programs.

Technology has made it possible for companies to compete in hiring high-priced technicians and skilled telemarketers, not to mention other talented workers, by enabling them to work at home. Once these individuals have joined the organization, however, only a few companies have been savvy enough to implement training programs to prepare both distance workers and their supervisors to manage well the new work relationship – organizations like AT&T and Corning, for example.

Where training is provided, it is designed to help managers make the tough decision about whether telecommuting makes business sense. If so, supervisors are then taught the skills to manage the work better, including fairly assessing work performance.

Among the issues that managers are asked to consider before committing to telecommuting are the following.

» What are the benefits of telecommuting? I mentioned earlier the benefit of making it easier to recruit and retain talented workers. But letting employees work at home can also cut the cost of office space. So there are questions to ask: Are office space costs going up sufficiently to justify telecommuting? Would telework make a real difference in overhead – that is, could office space be sublet, or could space currently being used be reallocated to areas where there is anticipated growth in staff?

» Are there jobs under your supervision that could be done more efficiently off-site than in the office? Would there be employee backlash if holders of these jobs were given the option of working at home and other employees had to continue to work in the office?

» Have any employees raised this issue with you yet? If so, are they individuals you would trust to work at home? If you agreed to their request, could you anticipate similar requests from others?

» Would commuting be an issue that could be addressed with telework? How about accessibility to a larger pool of employees? Would telework mean that you would have access to skills that currently are unavailable to you because of the location of either your company or the skilled workforce?

Let's assume that you come to the conclusion that telecommuting makes good business sense.

Managing the performance of telecommuters – that is, practicing distance management – really is no different from good supervision. To make it work in a department, all a supervisor need to do is to apply the basics of good performance management to remote employees. The supervisor manages not via observation but on the basis of results. Employees are managed as if they are adults who appreciate their responsibilities and can be trusted to carry them out unless they give their manager evidence to the contrary.

Managers practice performance management with off-site employees very much like they do every employee.

» Set clear expectations. This means that employees have a clear idea of what results each job is to achieve. Just as a manager would set key results or outcomes or standards with an on-site employee, he or she should set these expectations with an off-site worker. Standards in both cases are in writing.

   A telecommuter's agreement spells out both the organization's and the telecommuter's rights and responsibilities. For instance, who will be responsible for upkeep of any equipment (computer, fax, printer) required by the telecommuter?

» Agree on performance standards. What will a good job look like? Make the measurements as quantifiable as possible. When output can't be measured in numbers, you and the remote employee need to be positive you are in agreement on what the standards mean. Again, this mirrors the process a manager already should be following with on-site employees.

» Agree on how results will be monitored. Since the manager can't look outside his or her door to see how busy staff is, agreement on how work will be measured is critical.

   What reporting methods will be used – written or verbal reports, computer tracking, phone, or face-to-face meetings? How frequent will these be?

» One area managers will want to monitor is Internet activity. It is very easy for remote workers to become Internet junkies, caught up in the Information Superhighway. So managers need to include in the standards set what level of use will be considered an abuse of the communications technology.

» Provide feedback on performance. The manager needs to provide ongoing feedback to on-site employees. He or she needs to do the same for his or her off-site employees. That feedback won't always be given in person. But it can still be provided by telephone or e-mail. If a real problem exists, the manager will want to call the employee into the office for a face-to-face conversation. Actually, the means by which the manager provides feedback isn't as important as its frequency and how specific a manager can be about offering advice to improve performance.

These interim progress reports supplement traditional appraisals in which the manager sits down with the remote worker and reviews in greater depth his or her performance. Base pay is a function of the work, experience of the job holder, and importance of the position to the organization. Additional pay (e.g., merit increases, variable pay) is a reflection of job performance.

» Build trust. Since managers won't have the same control over telecommuters as they have over employees who work beside them, managers have to rely on the remote control that comes from employee respect. Managers can begin to foster that trust by showing that they trust their employees unless evidence proves that they can't. Managers need to operate on the assumption of trust, not distrust. Question only when they have real reason to do so – which is what today's outstanding traditional supervisors do anyway, right?

When it comes to keeping communication lines intact, here's a tip I heard from one manager to maximize communication, which is often more via phone than in person or through e-mail. Prepare for the meeting by developing "talking points," a list of those issues that you plan to address. You might also want the employee to e-mail or fax to you his or her "talking points" before the meeting. This way you are both prepared for the issues to be discussed. Time isn't wasted as one or the other of you hunts through desk files for the relevant piece of information that is being discussed.

» Fine-tune your listening skills. Whether an individual is in the office or on the phone, a manager wants to give him or her full attention. Even if the manager could read a report while talking to the telecommuter on the phone, he or she needs to put down the paperwork and concentrate on what the employee is saying. Show the person the respect he or she deserves by not doing anything else when you're on the phone with him or her. After all, you may discover a problem in the making or, better yet, some new source of income or operating tip that you can share with other remote workers.

While we talk about the benefits that the new office technology have brought to communication, we can't forget to mention the negative impact on work conditions – the physical discomforts like eye strain, wrist strain, and back strain, and also stress-related headaches of employees who have discovered that the cost of the new technology is the inability ever to be truly away from the office (think pagers, beepers, and cell phones). The new technology has also made work life more troubling by providing corporations with an arsenal of new tools to monitor the work performance of white-collar workers. They have traditionally enjoyed greater latitude than their blue-collar brethren regulated by tools such as time cards and assembly-line monitors. But today there are business software packages that can record how many keys are stroked, mouses clicked, and commands entered by each employee during a day. Call it desktop surveillance. While some people might argue that these monitors are not all that different from time records maintained by accountants, lawyers, and the like, the comparison is anything but apt, since too often these software packages are installed without the knowledge of the employees. Some systems produce such comprehensive records of computer activity that an employer can read every single thing a person types at the office – whether or not he or she stores the information in the computer's hard drive, prints it out, sends it to someone via e-mail, or deletes the record.

IT people will talk about the need to secure data. When the information is used to evaluate performance, management argues that it is for purposes of increasing employee efficiency. But some business writers have suggested that such control systems have only contributed further to creation of office sweatshops, given today's lean staffs with ever-increasing responsibilities.

When we talk about software packages, we can't forget mention of the new performance appraisal software also now available for good or evil. These new programs are designed to make it easier for managers to document performance by providing a variety of templates and text for producing reviews, even built-in legal checkers that highlight questionable terms like *attitude* or *old*. But these software programs all share a flaw: they ignore the objectives, standards, and work outcomes that are the foundation of the performance management process. Because the text is developed for so many applications, it does not work accurately for any single job, and consequently records kept about an employee's performance and the appraisal itself too often have little meaning. This weakens the strength of the manager's feedback during the one-on-one interview that is part of every performance evaluation.

Such software packages allow an employee to claim that the appraisal is nothing more than a point 'n' click document without any real thought or deliberation about the quality of work performed. Which may be a legitimate question about such packages. The software may in fact make documenting and conducting performance appraisals too easy. Thinking about the performance of an employee over the course of a year's accomplishments, assessing the worth of that performance, struggling to find the best performance – all may be difficult but that may be the way it should be if the assessments are to be fair and accurate descriptions of employee performance.

So this application of computer technology to performance appraisals may be better not used. On the other hand, there are other applications that are beneficial, as human resources has discovered. For instance, the corporate intranet can provide reminders to managers about quarterly or trimester reviews and serve as the vehicle for computer-based training on performance management, from setting goals or standards to maintaining documentation, to conducting effective appraisal interviews. They can also deliver training. Companies can combine classroom teaching with real work projects and knowledge databases using the Internet as a delivery channel. Individualized instruction to fill performance gaps can be made available any time via the intranet.

According to a study conducted by The Delphi Group, 16% of organizations used portals in early 1999. By the end of 2001, that figure had grown to over 80%.

HR software provides a range of analytical capabilities, from advanced reporting to sophisticated analysis. Among the packages available are those that cover:

» *compensation and benefits planning*: this tracks individual employees as well as groups to spot trends in the organization and also helps to answer what-if questions that will enable a company to develop the appropriate compensation and benefits program;
» *competency management*: this tracks skill levels of employees, then develops compensation and training to match workers' and organizational needs;
» *payroll programs*: this manages the entire payroll process, including regulations, tax considerations, and deductions; and
» *enterprise resource planning*: a systems package, this retains records, including performance appraisal reviews, automates processes, and links various functions or departments, allowing data to be shared across the organization.

As the Web has become more reliable, companies have increasingly turned to application service providers to host software and manage it from remote computers. Companies have found that, done right, ASPs do not hinder performance and eliminate up-front capital costs associated with buying systems.

Already most major human resources software products, including SAP, PeopleSoft, Lawson Software, Infinium, and Interlynx, are available through ASPs.

Portals and the Web are changing the way organizations manage human resources and the programs tied to them. Managers and employees can now directly access information and make on-the-spot decisions about employment, development, and pay without involving the HR function. The biggest development over the past several years on the technology front is the Web-based HR information portal, where sets of templates – including performance appraisal forms – can be accessed, completed, and then digitally submitted to HR for processing.

The emergence of intranets with HR portals and self-service technologies has created a major means for more easily managing performance and rewards. Managers can more easily complete their responsibilities in overseeing employee performance. And HR managers will be freed from spending time pushing paper.

A JUICY SOLUTION TO HR'S PAPERWORK PROBLEM

Morinda Inc., a Provo, Utah-based multi-level marketing firm, harvests, processes, and flavors Tahitian Noni Juice and distributes it to the United States and 19 other countries. Only six years old, the company reportedly made over $290mn in the year 2000. Founded by Kerry Asay, the company experienced rapid growth, with over 1000 salaried employees, about half of them outside the United States.

The last was a problem. As a global competitor, Asay couldn't afford to have his four-person human resources department buried in unnecessary paperwork. Until October 1999, the department was managing personnel records, payroll, benefits, and purchasing records the old way – on simple Microsoft Excel spreadsheets and other manual systems. Employee information was often entered several times – once for payroll, again for benefits, and a third time for performance reviews.

So the company turned to Oracle Corporation's software to handle its paperwork needs. By automating database management, the company was able to save both time and money. "We had to have something that supports our growth and keeps us integrated around the world," says Russ Wood, senior manager of corporate information systems.

Wood was looking for a software system that would be flexible, easy to maintain, and easy to use. "We were a high-growth company with multinational requirements," said Wood.

Oracle's software enabled management of records related to various activities.

» *Human resources*. Human resources could adopt structured approaches to attracting, retaining, and developing good employees.

» *Payroll*. The global payroll management system enables human resources to quickly and easily process many payrolls in a single day. The payroll engine allows rapid response to changes in pay and benefits policies and also enables the organization to provide year-end reports and fulfill government record keeping requirements.

» *Training administration*. The software handles a full range of business activities tied to training and development, scheduling events, and managing and scheduling resources required to deliver the training, as well as defining training activities. Thus HR is able to improve the abilities of its employees to meet current and future job needs in a cost-effective, focused manner.

» *Self-service HR*. Managers and employees could update and use people information through interfaces personalized to their roles and information needs.

In making his decision, it helped Wood to know that Oracle Corporation uses a similar system itself. Its HR organization manages programs for employees in more than 50 countries overseas. The employees speak in dozens of different languages, are compensated in many different currencies, and have cultural and local differences too varied to count. In 1999, when Wood installed its system at Morinda, Oracle was recruiting an average of 10% annually, yet HR was running a zero-growth budget, according to Joyce Westerdahl, Oracle's senior vice president of human resources. "In past years, our budget would have called for a growth rate in HR staff of half of the growth rate of the employee population." But with its new self-service functions, Oracle had been able to maintain a zero growth rate in some areas.

As Oracle itself experienced when it implemented a similar system, the biggest problem Morinda experienced was in inputting the information. Although Morinda had used Excel spreadsheets, the other information required for the HRMS system has been stored in paper files. "We spent hours gathering the material," according to Gary Williams, HR manager at Morinda. But once the information had been entered, they were on their way.

Efficiencies come from alerts that tell HR when an employee's status changes so all the benefit changes can be made quickly. It also allows for fewer mistakes in entering benefit payroll deductions. The company previously had made such calculations itself. Plans include further expansion of the computerized system, especially its self-service and Web functions.

What does this case study at Morinda tell us?

1 Automate when there are obvious cost and time savings.

2 Begin simply. Morinda took a conservative road, implementing only personal records, payroll, and benefits options. Once it was confident these were working as anticipated, it looked to the next stage, increasingly allowing HR managers to focus on the people issues that can't be done by a computer.

3 Seek out a system that meets your company's needs. Morinda went to Oracle to handle its computerization of HR data records. But there are other software programs. To get the best bang for your corporate buck, investigate those that will meet your needs to make the best purchase choice – including not only purchase price but payment to the software provider for sustaining the system.

The Global Dimension

This chapter outlines the factors that influence performance management and reward systems in global organizations.

Also check this chapter for information on:

» the role of variable pay around the world;
» the impact of culture and traditional differences on performance management; and
» payroll and performance issues for expats.

Just as products, services, and advertising must be tailored to diverse international markets, so too must performance management. When it comes to performance improvement, one cannot generalize from one region of the world to another region. Further, it isn't as simple today as it was a few years ago, as immigration changes the cultural makeup of countries. In 1993, *Time* magazine reported the following developments: one out of four babies born in Brussels was Arab; whole parts of the Paraguayan capital of Asunción were Korean; there were 40,000 "Canadian" residents in Hong Kong, many of whom spoke Cantonese as a first language; and almost half of the world's Mormons lived outside the US.

Culture isn't the only factor that needs to be considered. Gender equally influences opportunities worldwide. There is a story about a course that was pilot-tested in Nepal with prominent, well-educated, and well-traveled representatives of organizations from Nepal, Sri Lanka, Bangladesh, the Philippines, and India. There were fifty men and three women in the class. The instructor soon discovered that women would have to be specifically invited to attend field trips and that the women who did attend would have to be called on in class to give their opinions because their male counterparts would not give them an opportunity to participate. The instructor was from the United States but female, but the men were very respectful. As the instructor learned, the men would be attentive to anyone from the United States, regardless of the person's age or gender. On the other hand, had the same course been taught in Italy, where seniority and age are critical, the instructor might not have received the respect she did. There are other elements as well – like attitudes – within countries around the world that will influence the approach of companies within these countries to performance management and reward management.

Let's look at attitudes in Europe in comparison to those in the United States, for instance. In the United States, during the boom days, there was much gratification about the increase in productivity – even with its impact on the life of the typical US manager, who found balancing work/family life all but impossible given the work pressures. As European companies eyed the burgeoning increase in productivity in the US, the average European, including many a manager, regarded the American "productivity miracle" with concern. Who *wants* a life like that, no matter what the money? was the reaction of many, as they protectively tucked their six-week vacation into a cozy mental corner. Still, performance improvements that fostered US growth are seeping into Europe, despite union entrenchment.

Companies are slimming down by using attrition to reduce staff. (Layoffs are much more difficult to bring about in most European countries, under law.) A survey conducted by Britain's *Pay and Benefits Bulletin* in 2000 showed a decided uptick in companies planning to augment base pay with "competency-based pay," although there was less interest in skill-based pay. Profit sharing was one of the least considered strategies for the year ahead. The number of companies planning to offer some form of stock-ownership increased "markedly." Intriguingly, the significant increase in employers interested in incentive pay reported in 1999 flattened out. Those using the strategy stayed with it, but few new organizations planned on introducing it.

Around the world, wherever items are being manufactured or assembled, *pay for performance* will make its way into businesses currently paying employees for "piecework." A carefully designed and administered plan could be useful in developing countries for improving worker attitudes, compensation, and lifestyles, while reducing faulty products. The jury is out whether plans in developing countries will be designed with sufficient insight to avoid a potential pitfall (detriment to teamwork and overall employee cohesiveness, etc.).

One American export that likely will show global corporate popularity is the application of *worldwide standards of performance* and more centralized control at headquarters of evaluation and monitoring. Most global companies are organized on a regional basis. Managers run their regions within the cultural parameters of that region. That is changing. The speed with which data can now be assembled and transmitted to headquarters means top management can monitor and compare performance among regions on a timely basis. Thus if MyCore Corp. in Europe can sell 100,000 hearts a month, why can't MyCore/LatAm do the same? (There may, indeed, be reasons ... but top management will want to know them so they can be factored into the standards.)

Oracle is a case in point. Even this epitome of modern, Internet management initially set up its international business with each region operating much as a profit center that reported back to headquarters. The software giant soon realized that the flood of data being assembled on a regional basis could be centralized and quickly compared at headquarters, thus enabling the company to set worldwide standards.

Setting a "standard" worldwide for performance management in general will not be as easy. Just as compensation management is fragmented worldwide in response to local conditions and laws, other areas of performance management are equally dependent on the law or culture of the country. An Asian employee can be held to the same standards of performance as an American worker, but clearly, in a country where "saving face" is extremely important in human relations, the assessment must be handled differently. Similarly, the means of identifying problems and comparing employee performance country by country is the same, but how the problems are resolved differs. "Counseling" an underperforming employee in Germany or France takes on new challenges with the threat of termination spectral at best. Labor laws in these countries make terminating an employee extremely difficult – and expensive.

WHAT IS HAPPENING SPECIFICALLY GLOBALLY WITH COMPENSATION?

A study by consulting firm Towers Perrin found leading companies are increasingly developing similar approaches in their global compensation and benefit strategies. "As companies expand into new markets, employers find themselves increasingly searching for talented employees with global skills," said Fabrizio Alcobe-Fierro, a senior consultant in Towers Perrin's Global Resources Group. "New roles, responsibilities, and competencies drive the need to develop more consistent global strategies in concert with reward practices worldwide, with companies finding that global compensation and benefit strategies can achieve cost savings through economies of scale."

One major factor contributing to the convergence of global corporate compensation trends is the heightened transparency of pay practices as a result of employees' ready access to information about what competitors are paying. Another influence is the demand by employees for internal equity between comparable executive positions in different countries. Non-global local and regional competitors then must emulate practices of their global competitors. Countries that use the euro as the currency unit are also expected to find cost-of-living differences gradually becoming more transparent as exchange rate adjustments disappear and prices and currencies converge. No question, the practices of successful global companies with leading-edge strategies devoted to attracting employees and brand loyalty will be emulated by local and regional competitors.

Even with these factors, globalization of compensation won't erase important tax, accounting, and legal issues in individual countries. Said Jeffrey Schwartz, another senior consultant in Towers Perrin's Global Resources Group, convergence doesn't mean conformity. The best practices will demonstrate a pragmatic awareness of each country's existing cultural, historic, and social policies. Which means that global compensation and benefit approaches must be translated into effective design, implementation, and communication programs compatible with local market practices.

For instance, the study showed that the mix of pay components at companies is shaping up along similar lines as company compensation packages focus more on equity and individual performance. Base salaries comprise less of the total remuneration, especially when pay mix is evaluated within regions. For example, base salaries for senior positions in most European countries today represent 45% to 55% of total remuneration whereas they used to account for nearly 60% of total remuneration several years ago.

Strategies used to deliver pay are becoming more uniform from one country to the next. This trend is evident in two powerful types of variable pay – bonuses linked to individual performance and long-term incentive programs, especially stock-based plans. "Compensation and benefit packages that were once only familiar to executives are becoming increasingly available in some meaningful way to other employees within the organization," said Alcobe-Fierro.

Salary movements for CEOs, on average for all countries studied, show that base salary and perks decreased from 1996 to 2001 when expressed as a percentage of total remuneration. Long-term incentives, meanwhile, posted a noticeable increase as companies increased use of stock option programs. Reliance on base salary for mid-level managers eased while variable bonuses edged higher.

Towers Perrin's Worldwide Total Remuneration study also shows that companies in most countries are giving variable bonuses to professional staff or middle management and, in some cases, to manufacturing employees, extending a form of pay that used to apply only to senior executives. "The challenge for companies is ongoing," according to Alcobe-Fierro. "When it comes to a total remuneration strategy, most companies want to 'get it right' by pulling together the strands that work best globally, while finding ways to differentiate themselves as competitors."

What does this mean in real money? According to the Tower Perrin study, 28% of annual remuneration of a CEO in the US is from base pay, 61% is from variable pay, and the remaining 11% is made up of perks and benefits. In the United Kingdom, on the other hand, 43% is base pay, 30% is variable pay, and the remaining 27% is for perks and benefits. How does this compare with Latin American firms? A CEO in Argentina makes 47% of his or her pay from base, 43% from variable pay, and the remaining 10% from perks and benefits. In Japan, on the other hand, as much as 59% is base pay. Only 18% is variable pay. 23% is made up of perks and benefits. In Germany, the situation is more comparable to the US and other countries, in which 47% is from base pay, 36% from variable pay, and the remaining 17% from perks and benefits.

For CEO remuneration for each country, variable pay includes long-term incentive pay for 2001 that was not evident in 1996, as mentioned.

Let's look at the next level down, to the position, say, of accountant. If we look at the same countries, someone in that position in the US would receive 76% of his pay as base pay, only 4% from variable pay, and the remaining 20% as benefits. In the United Kingdom, 60% of an accountant's salary would be base pay. 11% would come from variable pay. Perks and benefits would make up the remaining 21%. In Germany, the breakdown would be: 80% base pay, 20% in benefits, more comparable to the US. In Japan, only 2% is designated as variable pay. Base pay accounts for 77% of pay. 21% is made up of benefits.

In Argentina, 77% of total remuneration came in base pay. Three percent was in the form of variable pay. And the remaining 20% was for benefits. As mentioned, for middle level managers reliance on base salaries eased while variable bonuses edged upward.

Going down further, there was even evidence that variable pay was being given to some manufacturing employees, although the number of countries doing so were few (e.g., Taiwan, Thailand, Singapore, New Zealand, Hong Kong, Brazil, and Australia).

So we can expect performance management practices to reflect cultural issues more often than not around the world. On the other hand, global compensation and benefit strategies seem increasingly to be built around similar philosophies to incentivize performance with variable short- and long-term pay. Clearly the most successful companies worldwide will be those that can combine a pragmatic awareness of the culture of the country in which they operate with effective design, implementation, and communication programs for their pay practices.

The State of the Art

In this chapter, learn how companies are:

» maximizing motivational value of their performance management programs;

» using non-monetary rewards where dollars are limited; and

» incorporating variable pay increasingly into all employees' pay plans.

In early 1999, with the economy roaring ahead and unemployment licking at 4%, management articles rang with odes to "retaining and motivating employees in a competitive marketplace." In 2001 the economy entered into a recession, and companies already lean from previous cutbacks sucked in their corporate belts even further, trimming off any tiny bit of excess employee fat, passing on the work to the remaining staff. The business press focused on "how to wring the most out of your workforce." Today, companies that once gave freely of dollars and praise to find and keep talented workers continue to conduct performance assessments. Some may give variable pay in the form of bonuses, and there are some that continue to give merit rewards but at percentage points that mean little in terms of stimulating high performance, but increasingly companies are forgoing raises at all. Indeed, there are companies that have taken to pay cutbacks for purposes of survival or time off without pay.

When it comes to the broader issue of management of people, the backsliding economy highlights a corporate trend first evidenced some 10 years ago – a kind of "tough love" performance management. Monitoring, evaluation, counseling, training – the basic skills remain the same. But the manner in which the skills are applied and the emphasis on one skill over another is changing in response to the specific culture of the organization and a work climate that is described variously as "empowering" or "demanding," depending on whether the speaker is positive or negative about the evolution.

How companies view labor has shifted: from "training and retaining" marginal employees (partly in response to social and government pressures and partly to expand a shrinking labor supply) to quickly monitoring and strengthening an underachiever's performance or out the door they go. A performance management process of evaluation, response, feedback, etc., that a few years back might have moved along at a stately pace for six months or a year before management helped a chronically underachieving employee to wend her way gracefully out the corporate door, nowadays might zip to an end in weeks.

Sound harsh? Not in a world where companies like Oracle and Cisco rely on evaluations in part to lop off the bottom 5% to 10% of their workforce each year. Just routine, ma'am. True, employees are given a chance to upgrade performance, but it has to be thorough, fast, and a good fit, or they catch the scythe.

This posture toward tough-minded high performance might seem a contradiction in light of the anticipated shortage of skilled workers, as predicted by the US Department of Labor. Managers are expected to train, support, and motivate employees to bring them up to peak performance. They will even be evaluated themselves on their coaching capability. Yet they also are being asked to make tough termination decisions that over the short term will lower the productivity of their work team as they train replacements who may or may not be equal in performance to those being let go.

True, not every company is operating with the aggressiveness of a high-risk/high-reward company like Oracle or Cisco. But there is no question that companies are adjusting their performance management posture. Even their reward management posture is increasingly under-going change. Managers are expected to coach employees to achieve a high-performance workforce. Their goal is to create a workforce in which all members are superior in a few years' time. Employees who don't make the cut will be asked to leave, and their departure will be preceded by sound, rigorous documentation. No lawsuits, thank you.

In the United States, to minimize the danger of lawsuits due to termination for cause, increasingly companies are implementing termi-nation at will policies to give them the freedom to terminate employees without the time and trouble to justify the termination due to problem performance.

This response to bad times is very different from previous downturns. Prior to the 1980s, companies responded to hiccoughs in the economy in an almost lockstep, binge-starve manner. Recession: lay off 10 employees. Upturn: hire back 12. Recession: let go 15 people. Upturn: hire 30. Not this last time. As the economy started to heat up in the 1990s, companies ran lean. If a US firm added people, it was for the purpose of growing a new area of business. (Some economists claim the following eight years' boom resulted from the increased productivity that helped produce record corporate profits. Possible. Opponents of that view point to 2001 government downward revisions of the productivity and GDP numbers for the 1998–99 period, and align the growth rate more with expansions of previous cyclical upswings rather than as "a productivity miracle.") Deeper into the 1990s, companies started to change how they paid, to more clearly reflect the employee's contributions. Pay for performance was the rallying call of chief financial officers. Variable pay programs more frequently augmented or modified the pay package. They went from being a part of only the total compensation of senior executives to being a part of the pay plans of all managers and employees, including administrative assistants and facilities workers. Merit increases still existed but the percentage was so low – averaging around 4% or $27.00 more per week for an employee earning $50,000 per year – no one seriously thought it would affect one's level of performance.

Bonuses or incentive pay are replacing raises as rewards for good work. Some companies have eliminated automatic raises altogether.

Companies realize that money is still very much a motivator. It's why most people go to work. Thus it is a vital component of motivating or demotivating employees to perform their jobs well. Maybe pay is tied to widgets produced (with quality), maybe to ratings of managerial "competencies," or some other measure. Adherents point to creating a work atmosphere where stars can shine and are rewarded for their superior contributions, where no employee is "entitled" to a paycheck, and morale is boosted along with productivity because solid workers no longer have to put up with co-workers who don't pull their weight. Lisa Weber, MetLife's executive vice president of human resources, claims in the August 2001 issue of *Workforce* magazine that their pay for performance program has "been tough, but it's been fabulous."

Opponents of the plans agree that exceptional workers should be rewarded, but in another manner. Pay for performance programs, they claim, create an atmosphere that is antithetical of teamwork (Remember "teamwork," the buzzword of organizational dynamics only a few years ago?) Opponents of pay for performance say it forces competition between "team mates," fosters envy, and undermines group efforts. The same magazine article quotes the chairman of Lantech, a manufacturer of packaging machinery, as scuttling the company's pay for performance program because of the divisiveness it caused among "rival gangs of workers." Further, opponents say programs have the potential to devolve into fancy sweatshops. There is even speculation that in some future economic downturn companies will strip away the financial incentives that accompany the increased production, leaving only "production quotas" and the right to keep your job.

The opponents question the findings of behaviorists about the value of the carrot in performance. They point to various studies that found people who are trying to earn a reward doing a poorer job on many tasks than people who are not. When does pay for performance fall short? According to Stanford University Professor Jeffrey Pfeiffer, when it pits employees against each other. Pfeiffer has researched the subject extensively and declares the idea of pay for performance "a myth." According to Pfeiffer, "A company's success is not a consequence of what an individual does. It's a consequence of what the system does." Pfeiffer says evidence indicates that incentive pay may be more effective at a divisional or organizational level – in the form of profit sharing, stock ownership, gain sharing, and group bonuses – than an individual level. Marc Holzer, a Rutgers University business professor and president of the American Society for Public Administration, has found individual incentive plans do more damage than good.

Holzer has watched agencies and schools implement performance-based pay schemes, try them out, keep them, change them, and then abandon them. "They set up competition between people. They emphasize the individual rather than the team. Virtually all innovations are group efforts. Yes, the exceptional person should be rewarded. But that exceptional person is dependent on others, on support services, which is often ignored." According to Pat Lancaster, of Lantech, "Incentive pay is toxic. By the early 1990s, I was spending 95% of my time on conflict resolution instead of how to serve our customers."

Opponents of pay for performance point to the success in competitor countries of the US, like Japan and Germany, where pay for performance is not the standard.

A Hewitt Associates study released in the year 2000 gave pay for performance mixed results. More companies are using the incentive plan now than a decade before but only 22% said they believed that the pay incentives were working. Only 57% said that it "somewhat helped." An earlier Hewitt survey, conducted in 1995, found that among the 61% of organizations in the same year that had adopted variable compensation plans with budgets of $5mn or more, 48% of the plans failed to achieve their goals.

The jury is still out, but the likelihood is strong that an increasing number of companies will try *some version of incentive pay*. Companies today are searching for *some way* to tie performance to pay. A 1999 survey by publisher IOMA reported that the improvement most desired by compensation managers was a move to variable pay packages. Hewitt Associates reported in 2000 that more companies were using versions of pay for performance than 10 years earlier, but only 22% believed pay incentives work. In fact, 21% thought they didn't help. 57% thought they "somewhat helped."

Opponents believe that intrinsic motivation is more likely to generate increased performance – internal motivators like pride in one's work, the challenge of solving difficult problems, and greater participation in decisions – than extrinsic rewards. But this isn't likely to put an end to structured programs.

Whatever form these plans take, they will require a tighter, *more structured and objective performance measurement system*. *More monitoring* will be required (likely computerized), and *rigorous documentation*. Managers will need *training* in the components of the process, as well as in coaching. It's unclear whether the organization-wide increase in (computerized) paperwork and time will justify potential gains, but it *is* clear that the human resource manager, working with line and staff managers, will be responsible for designing, maintaining, and administering a more complex system.

The idea behind pay for performance is that an employee will put out more effort when there's something in it for him. The trick of designing the programs, say consultants, is to tie the employee's goals to the company's goals. With this in mind, more companies are offering employees stock ownership in some form – ESOPs, stock contributions to IRAs, or outright stock options. In the United States, in 1998, 34% of employees of major US corporations owned stock in the companies they worked for. Arguably, dot-coms escalated the stock-ownership trend – a trend that moved beyond the US borders as dot-coms grew around the world. Young techies accepted low base pay in return for stock options that could be exercised when the company went public. The lure of a big reward motivated many to put in long hours and to perform well.

The appeal was clear, and increasingly mainstream performance management programs incorporated stock options for lower-level managerial employees. The danger is now just as clear. The plans are less appealing in a down market. Further, many of those same techies – just as talented but a bit older and wiser – would not today accept pay arrangements that did not include a livable and competitive base salary.

When new productivity or pay plans are introduced, employees may be leery of the change and cynical about its purpose. Many leading-edge performance professionals are enlisting the aid of communications specialists not just to prepare written, complete explanations of new performance programs and to conduct workshops, but to help *create an atmosphere of openness and trust in what's being proposed* so employees are less fearful of the changes. Understanding how the company operates, its profit picture, prospects, and why it's making the changes, provides employees with a fuller picture. Some companies are experimenting with enlisting *employees in designing their own pay and productivity improvement plans*, as a way to get them to "buy" the final package. Communication experts also suggest allowing employees time to adjust to the thought and implementation of the new plan. Most important, of course, is fostering a true understanding of how the plan will benefit each employee individually.

The manager is the point person who implements and monitors the plan and supervises employee performance. Increasingly, she is being *assessed officially* on competency in coaching employees to incrementally higher performance. Designing objective parameters to monitor how well a manager supervises is a challenge. Clever people find ways to thwart clever performance managers. Author David Banks reports in *Breaking Windows: How Bill Gates Fumbled the Future of Microsoft*[1] how some supervisors would get themselves transferred to departments where the performance bar wasn't as high as other areas of the company. Other line managers, knowing they'd be judged by their subordinates' performance, clearly padded their luck by having only *superior* subordinates.

Which brings up the "total evaluation" – the 360. The round-the-world evaluation appears to be decreasing in use. The concept held the promise of a more complete picture of an employee's performance, as it evaluated him from below, above, alongside and, occasionally, from a bird's eye customer view. The concept leaves out the common-sense and self-protective way human beings operate. The promised confidentiality is pretty thin; most employees can gauge the identity of their evaluators. Will subordinates share their *real* opinions . . . and open the door to retaliation from the boss next year? Does the boss who rated his subordinate well on the yearly evaluation at raise time revise that assessment in a 360 and bring up matters never discussed before because she feels it won't affect salary? This must produce some confusing and conflicting feelings in the employee.

The most serious glitches turn up with peers. How do you keep from running a popularity contest? How do you keep colleagues from agreeing to go soft on one another? Worse: what if one manager seriously (and with a touch of negativity) evaluates her peer manager – who says the adjudged manager won't subtly retaliate by withholding cooperation on joint department ventures?

Three-sixties were the newest wrinkle in performance management only a decade ago. They proved useful in team relationships in disclosing "surprise opinions" from colleagues and in opening dialogue. They were the product of the "team age."

Already there have been considerable changes in performance and reward management. But we can expect more to occur as the world of work itself changes. For one, performance management needs to devise new means of assessing workers who work outside the headquarters building – for example, employees who work from home or a field location. How will companies monitor and assess the growing numbers of "distance workers?" Judging solely by results might work for a sales manager, but how about an editor? One company located in Maryland hired an editor in California to produce a newsletter once a month. The company specified the contents, delineated the audience and deadlines. Only the length of the newsletter was never determined. The California editor, who seldom contacted headquarters, turned out one 4-page newsletter each month. Was this satisfactory? To set reasonable job standards, management needs an objective measure of how long the work should take.

Few distance workers contribute significantly to team effort – brainstorming, intrapreneurial concepts, special projects. Should their contribution be assessed differently from that of headquarters staff? If the distance employee's work is satisfactory, but could be better, how does management coach and counsel? If the distance worker is considered a "special talent," what effect does this have on the "special talents" who work at headquarters and are called on to staff teams, attend meetings, work on special projects?

At present, most companies evaluate distance workers in the same manner as headquarters employees. As their numbers swell, performance managers will likely be called on to set up more objective parameters, tighter measurements and controls by which to standardize and improve their productivity.

One group of workers that currently falls almost completely outside the zone of structured performance appraisals is contract workers. This includes temporary and freelance help, as well as workers who are subcontracted to the company by a third-party organization. This group has traditionally been regarded as expedient, handy workers to use when short-staffed or when full-time workers were unavailable, and they were rated simply as "satisfactory" or "unsatisfactory." If the latter, they were replaced with new warm bodies.

The role of the contract worker changed in the 1990s. One way companies stayed lean was by using "temporary" staff, which sometimes wasn't so temporary. One company's union contract stipulated it could use a freelance person for only 90 days before filling the position with a full-time (union) member. The company simply rotated temporary workers, and hired a new temp for each spot every 90 days. Union membership wasn't strong enough for the union to force a change to this violation of the "spirit" of the agreement.

Temps, freelancers, and consultants each operate with various levels of professionalism, depending of course on the individual and the level of expertise required by the job.

As companies increasingly use contract workers and for extended periods of time, measurements and assessments will have to be constructed to measure, improve, and augment their performance. Contract workers may be cheaper, but if their work is inferior to staff workers, they may be expensive at any price.

Lean staffs have also raised the profile – and value – of workers who can perform multiple jobs. No need to hire a temp … just move the multiskilled employee to the new location and let others in her department perform tasks for the interim.

Innovative programs that intentionally skill employees in many tasks have decided benefits to both the company *and* the employee. Being skilled in many areas makes the employee more valuable to his own employer as well as to a potential new employer. Further, rotation makes work more interesting, as the challenges change.

At Industrial Ceramic Products (ICP), the move from piecework to incentive-based pay was accompanied by a program that trained and rotated employees in various tasks. The plant's production operation requires about 40 tasks. All employees were trained up to perform additional tasks, and were rotated daily, though not all employees were rotated into all tasks, as they required different levels of skill. The most desirable slots required specialized skills that were paid the most, thus employees wanted to learn the skill to be rotated into that task.

A prime determinant of ICP's decision to go from piecework to incentive pay was to control quality. Thus, the company designed a logging system to run in tandem with the skills-training program. Employees log each defective piece so managers can track quality and spot a consistent problem with skills or operations.

Job rotation isn't just for line workers. At one major news magazine secretaries are trained to replace vacationing or sick regular employees at the "newsdesk," the hub linking editors with overseas correspondents. Staff help correspondents file copy, fix transmission problems, track the whereabouts of the reporters, and keep them connected with their editors and researchers. They are the "lifeline" to the headquarters mother ship, on occasion even getting correspondents emergency help in war zones.

For the company, training secretaries to work at the newsdesk saves hiring a temp and puts the job in the hands of an employee who knows the "players" under deadline pressure. For the secretaries, working the newsdesk is job enrichment. They love the excitement of the job and learn marketable equipment skills.

Job rotation saves the company money, and it clearly perks up job satisfaction. But how does rotation affect assessments? Should the rotation be factored into job expectations? Are there union ramifications?

Job rotation is only one method to establish a win-win proposition for employees and the company. Increasingly, organizations are investigating *any mechanism that might increase productivity*. Ernst & Young is running a pilot project to retain more women professionals by helping them establish a more flexible and creative *"dual-life" work routine*. The firm claims client satisfaction has increased and it has saved $17mn. Kraft Foods' pizza plant in Sussix, Wisconsin, is one of a growing number of factories that encourage *employees to design or significantly contribute to the design of work schedules and procedures*. Its assembly-line employees devised a system that gave them more flexible and predictable work hours – better for them – and which also boosted production, reduced overhead costs and downtime, and improved turnover. Very good for Kraft. A study by the Work in America Institute in the Fall of 2000 claimed that "work/life initiatives are no longer viewed as employee perks, but more as strategic business tools linked to core corporate objectives, such as customer satisfaction, leadership development, and teamwork."

For employees, finding ways to balance non-work life with the workplace is becoming crucial. *Burnout and dropout* are two increasing responses to work and stress overload, and many of the employees dropping out of the "rat race" are talented professionals and very good performers. They are leaving the fast-track for "a life" – working for companies that do not operate routinely in overdrive. Performance managers in organizations heavily staffed with professionals are particularly sensitive to issues of burnout and dropout (read "employee turnover.") Their performance "problems" are less with increasing productivity than with keeping highly motivated workers in good health, good humor, and on the job.

Even in "saner" organizations, employees are working longer hours . . . and will continue to do so. Organizations are escalating the tendency to "detach" groups of professional and managerial employees to complete projects they formerly staffed up for or farmed out. Many times, new projects are simply piled on top of the manager's regular, very busy job. Though pay is still a prime motivator, these executives are negotiating *more leisure time – vacations, sabbaticals –* as trade-offs for the intense pace required by additional, short-term projects. Flexible benefits programs are growing in popularity; in many of them, employees can "buy" extra vacation. (One factor likely inhibiting their growth is the amount of record-keeping involved.)

What does all this mean to performance management and reward management?

The pace of work at the workplace is increasing. Many of the new processes aimed at boosting productivity require much *stricter and tighter measurements*. Further, many job descriptions will require revamping to include newer, broader *"expectations and goals"* at the management level. *Increased paperwork* (much of it computerized) will be a challenge, as *monitoring and documentation* will likely be heightened as performance management systems become more formalized. The means of *identifying* the performance problems will remain basically the same, but how these *behaviors* are monitored and *modified* will require additional training and procedures. In companies moving to incentive pay, *new administrative systems* will be required for *record-keeping and resolution of discrepancies*. *Training* will be needed for nonexempt workers – bringing the unskilled up to skilled and skilled to superior – and for managers whose new responsibilities will include incremental increases in the productivity of their staffs.

Perhaps the biggest challenge for managers will be to *find new ways to motivate employees*. As organizational psychologist Abraham Maslow pointed out in the 1960s with his "hierarchy of needs," humans have evolving motivators as they inch up the pyramid of achievement. Once food, shelter, warmth, sex and companionship, security, and the like are attained, they no longer motivate the human to exert extra energy. Enough years doing the same job on the same line numbs any worker, no matter what her pay. New incentives to up productivity need to be found.

Work redesign holds promise, as it gives employees some say over their work life. Flexible work schedules and informal work attire certainly do not appear to have hindered productivity, so companies may increasingly permit more latitude for employees to adjust work to suit their personal needs.

In some cases, work-personal adjustments may involve changing headquarters employees to distance workers. Performance management so far has stayed uninvolved in many issues of *distance management*, leaving local managers to deal with the particulars in each case.

But as the trend continues, performance professionals may be called on to formalize assessment and monitoring mechanisms for this group.

NOTE

1 Banks, D. (2001) *Breaking Windows: How Bill Gates Fumbled the Future of Microsoft*. Free Press, New York.

In Practice

Learn more in this chapter about corporate programs at companies like:

» AlliedSignal;
» Case Corporation;
» DuPont Corporation; and
» TRW.

To understand what makes for efficient, effective performance management and reward programs, let's look at some. In this chapter, we will focus on the programs at companies like:

» Behlen Manufacturing
» Robert Bosch Corporation
» GTE Telephone Operations
» Texas Instruments
» Case Corporation
» Sonoco

REWARDS TO BUILD TEAMWORK

At Columbus, Nevada-based Behlen Manufacturing, manufacturer of livestock equipment, grain storage and drying systems, and building systems, incentive systems begin with a program called Awareness Is Money that awards at least $250 monthly to the employee with the best idea about how to improve safety and productivity. But the real benefits come when the ideas are implemented and work – and productivity increases. Implementation is done in teams made up of from 10 to 30, and employees who participate in an idea's success from start to finish – like manufacture of a building team – can earn bonuses of up to 12% of their base pay. The bonuses are part of a monthly gain-sharing program. To build a sense of team throughout the organization, office employees as well as factory workers participate in the program.

Behlen also offers a profit-sharing plan in which rewards are given annually, based on profits made. In a good year, employees may receive as much as 140 hours of pay as a Christmas bonus.

Management installed these reward programs to create a more participatory culture. According to CEO Anthony Raimondo, the result has been tremendous employee loyalty and productivity. "Our employees are all in the business fight with us, so our theme is 'Make the company better off, and we will share.' " In Raimondo's view, management recognized that the firm couldn't achieve competitive advantage unless the company and everyone in it were committed to the company's goals, which meant that all had to share in the fruits of the organization's success.

Behlen's experience demonstrates the importance of reward programs having certain key factors in place.

» *Management support*: An organization's leadership has to see the relationship between corporate performance and employee creativity and productivity.
» *A variety of rewards*: Behlen offers a variety of ways to gain value-added from their job performance.
» *Rewards for team efforts*: Individuals within a winning team share equally in the benefits that come from implementation of a good idea – from start to finish.
» *Participation extended throughout the organization*: Office workers, as well as plant employees, were eligible for the rewards.

THE TRUE BENEFITS OF REWARD PROGRAMS

The economy has put added pressure on manufacturers to decrease costs and increase quality and product reliability. If the company is in the automobile manufacturing business, the demand is even greater. Which brings us to Robert Bosch Corporation, Anderson, South Carolina, an automobile original equipment manufacturer (OEM).

The company was a competitive player in the global marketplace but it realized that further improvements in productivity, costs, and customer responsiveness were needed. New work systems (like cross-training, teamwork, and increased employee autonomy) had been made but more change was needed, as of 1999.

The company suffered from a highly structured work environment in which associates (think "employees") worked at assigned stations and were familiar with only a given set of machines, and pay and performance management systems rewarded seniority and job titles, not performance. There were also limited career growth opportunities – very frustrating for the best performers. The only way to get a promotion was to bid for a higher-graded job, and new job openings prompted as many as 60 internal applicants.

Of course, when there were crew shifts, there were problems as a departing worker took his know-how about the shift's processes or products with him, which could cost in time, resources, and productivity. But worst of all, while the company conducted performance assessments, rewards were tied to a graded system. Employees also complained that the reviews were subjective or arbitrary. Since group leaders oversaw up to 60 employees, they had little opportunity to observe and assess each individual's work behavior.

Bosch came up with two answers: team-oriented production (TOP) and career banding.

Under TOP, operators were organized into teams and members were asked to take greater responsibility for quality and costs. To make this happen, the organization came up with six point positions – from point leader, to delivery point leader, to equipment point leader, to cost point leader, to quality point leader – and employees were assigned these on a six-month rotating basis. These roles required them to take ownership of these areas.

What about the limited opportunities for promotions or complaints about the performance reviews? The company replaced the labor grades with a performance management and development program that rewarded employees for their job proficiency. No longer did employees have to bid for open positions. Employees received regular feedback on their job performance and competencies required for personal growth.

For both operators and technicians, four performance levels were formed – entry, skilled, proficient, and advanced. Employees (aka associates) were given detailed matrices that showed performance criteria and proficiency levels for each level. Proficiency levels reflect workplace skills, including but not limited to department-specific skills. This detail is seen as crucial since it enables the firm's associates to see where there are skill gaps.

Reviews include development plans that allow employees to close gaps at their own pace. If employees think they are ready for an upgrade, they must pass an upgrade review conducted by a five-member panel before which the employee must demonstrate the skill. The panel consists of representatives from human resources, their colleagues, technicians, and engineers, and the employee's supervisor.

What have the results been to date? The company has experienced an excellent improvement in productivity – as high in some areas as 25% – and a reduction in defect costs of as much as 57% in three years. Further, overtime costs have dropped by over a third.

Career banding has also been successful. Promotions are based on skill progress and merit rather than a successful job bid.

What can be learned from Bosch's program?

Performance management/reward management programs aren't a single issue. The organization must be considered as a whole in planning the performance review program and tying it to financial or promotional rewards. Bosch tied it to effort to make employees own their responsibilities with skill-based performance management/rewards.

Linking performance management and performance development makes sense. Bosch conducted reviews to identify specific skill gaps and then gave employees the opportunity to demonstrate newly gained proficiency in these areas and receive rewards for doing so – from pay to promotions.

Bosch was focused on its internal culture. But appraisal programs also need to reflect national cultures. More and more companies that go global are recognizing the need to account for cultural differences. A case in point: DuPont.

As the company considered some form of incentive for information technology specialists from around the globe, it discovered just how different needs were. The staff in Japan said individual pay incentives would have limited worth – some even suggested negative repercussions – while those in another Asian culture found that individual incentives would be highly effective. The people from the European region valued one approach less than people in both South and North America. The answer for DuPont and many other global organizations has been to allow each region represented by its organization to decide what incentives it plans to offer. In DuPont's case, four plans are offered.

Companies have come to see compensation as a tool to be used for a specific purpose and to the extent that it will produce a return, there is a need for regional adaptation as well as adaptation to corporate needs.

TYING APPRAISALS TO CORPORATE MISSIONS

It isn't just tying compensation to corporate needs. Besides reward management, organizations tie appraisal systems to strategy. For example, GTE Telephone Operations has built its appraisal process around the seven values considered essential to achievement of competitive advantage: quality, benchmarking, people, market sensitivity, innovation, technology, and employee involvement and teamwork.

The company uses an appraisal form that lists several dozen short statements of anticipated performance. The assessor is expected to indicate both the importance of the skill or behavior – from critical to not applicable – and then the level of the employee's performance.

Some organizations, including PepsiCo and General Mills, have used values tied to mission to create 360-degree feedback forms for employee development as well as for purposes of assessment, thereby linking performance management and employee development.

NEW APPRAISAL MODELS

If there is a major shift in performance appraisals recently, it is who does the appraisal – and of whom.

At NRL Federal Credit Union, located in Oxon Hill, Maryland, employees complained that there was no relationship between organizational goals and individual performance, not to mention lack of feedback. A task force of managers and employees from throughout the organization was formed. It came up with a four-part approach. The first three parts are very familiar: job objectives or results written by both managers and employees, job behaviors perceived as critical to achievement of the organization's strategy, and technical skills that range from job knowledge to more general management skills like problem solving and decision making.

Peer evaluation is the unique part of the program. Peer evaluations focus on teamwork, initiative, and contribution to the work. Employees describe how colleagues either help or hinder them in doing their job, sharing specific examples. The process with which feedback is provided is also very different in that employees don't just complete a form but rather communicate feedback in one-on-one meetings.

The program also has employees giving feedback to supervisors. These aren't just facilitated discussions. Each employee rates his or her supervisor on a five-point scale – from outstanding to marginal – and then they provide an overall rating. According to Linda Steger, human resources manager for the firm, the reviews actually accurately reflect supervisory behavior. It isn't easy but research shows that supervisors are responsive – perhaps because the first task factor raised in the evaluation is active listening.

Nashville, Tennessee's Quorum Health Resources has given appraisals a new twist, too. Rather than have the appraisal process run by the supervisor, the process is actually done by the employee. Employees felt that customer feedback was the most important factor to assess, and that that feedback should be ongoing (not solely provided once a year). Nor were employees interested in a paper-driven system in which the supervisor checks boxes on a printed form. So here is the four-part program that the company inaugurated in 1990.

1 *Plan*: The employee and supervisor meet to determine who the employee's customers are, what information the employee will need to collect from them, and how the employee will collect the information. As employees gather input, one insightful piece of information from customers often is: what is the most important part of the individual's job?
2 *Information gathering*: The employee is encouraged to ask customers directly to evaluate his or her work and suggest ideas for improvement. That includes identification of organizational hindrances to job performance.
3 *Meeting*: Once the employee has completed his or her search for information, the individual shares it with the supervisor. They discuss what kind of improvement the information suggests needs to be made. From this comes a plan of action, with timetable, and agreement on how improvements will be measured.
4 *Evaluation*: The supervisor and employee decide on how the feedback session went and what, if anything, needs to be done about gathering information.

Where does pay come in? It doesn't. The firm uses prevailing market wage and skill-based increases to determine compensation changes. According to the company, employees didn't object to this change. Interestingly, they didn't even suggest intrinsic rewards – like praise and recognition. Rather, they asked for better and more resources to make it easier to do their jobs.

Any discussion of unique appraisal programs has to include Texas Instruments' Consumer Products Division that uses team-based peer assessments. The division uses a questionnaire with descriptive statements of team behavior. Members are asked to rate fellow team members in each. At first, the assessments were anonymous. After a while, however, the process was changed into a team development program with each member put in the hot seat for purposes of hearing feedback from peers. The same behaviors covered in the anonymous rating sheets were raised by team members during these sessions.

The hot seat occupant then was expected to address three questions.

1 What did people say about you?
2 What do you think about what was said?
3 What are you going to do about it?

Over time, the process has become even more sophisticated, with use of a form in which members rate peers both on good and bad points.

Clearly the intent of the process is open and honest communication to improve team performance.

What about compensation? Team rankings of individual members is used to determine percentage of reward.

These three examples suggest how there is no one format for appraisals. Clearly, however, they highlight several important points.

» *Feedback*: The best feedback may come not only from supervisors but from peers and customers (internal and external).
» *Pay shouldn't necessarily be tied to appraisals*: When pay is factored in, it makes receptivity to evaluation results more difficult for the hearer.
» *Needs determine form*: There is no single approach to performance management or reward systems.

COMPETENCY-BASED PERFORMANCE MANAGEMENT/REWARD SYSTEMS

We've examined some skill-based programs. Let's consider two companies with competency-driven performance management/reward programs:

Case Corporation

A leading designer, manufacturer, and distributor of agricultural and construction equipment, Case sells its products in over 150 countries through a network of more than 5000 independent dealers. In 1994, the company undertook research to develop two competency models – one for corporate leaders and another for individual contributors – both directly linked to the operating principles, strategic imperatives, and mission of Case. The intent was to integrate these models into performance management and development, 360-degree feedback and development planning, and human resource planning, including recruitment.

Specifically, the performance management and development effort supports yearly objective setting and assessments. Targeted interviewing, an element of competency modeling, enables managers to identify candidates who have the behaviors to meet business unit and corporate goals. 360-degree feedback specifies the behaviors that employees need, and the development side looks at ways to help those with deficiencies to fill skill, ability, or knowledge gaps. Human resource planning allows employees to talk about their career goals and managers to create succession plans tied to the competencies needed.

How does the program actually work? Employees are assessed against what they do and how they do it. Performance results or what an employee accomplishes are based on key results expected during the year. These objectives reflect the overall strategy of the company and business unit or division as they cascade down, based on business goals. The goals also include one or two developmental goals for each employee, often derived from the 360-degree assessments.

How the employee does is a measure of his or her supervisor and reflected in the leadership competency model, which includes specific behaviors required of good performance coaches, like: fosters open communication, develops others, practices team leadership. The components include a performance agreement completed at the beginning of the year and revised as necessary throughout the 12-month period. For development objectives, key actions required to achieve those are defined. Progress against set goals are measured at mid-year and year-end, but managers are expected to provide ongoing feedback. The competency assessment at year-end is a formal evaluation of the level at which each employee demonstrated every competency. The performance summary, then, combines the employee's performance in terms of competencies, performance results, and development compared to objectives.

If there is one point that stands out about Case's program it is the firm's effort to gain common understanding of the importance of competencies. Leaders, managers, and employees were all involved in the development of the competency models, either through interviews, focus groups, or validation surveys. It helped that the competency models, performance management tools and process, and 360-degree feedback programs were all tied together.

Sonoco

A 100-year-old packaging company, Sonoco has sales that top $2.6bn, with more than 18,000 employees in 300 different locations, on five continents and in 33 countries. It's hard to believe that a company can grow to that size by producing canisters used for snacks, cookies, or nuts or plastic bags used in grocery stores, but so it is.

The goal of Sonoco's performance management system is to help employees better understand their roles within the organization and, more important, align their performance in support of business goals. Employee development is a secondary goal. The present system replaced a 15-year-old program that was more event than process, characterized by infrequent training and plagued with meaningless numerical scores for evaluating employee's past performance. The current program is clearly process-oriented and focuses on the relationship between individual accomplishments and corporate results. The change, in 1995, also enabled Sonoco to develop a single performance management system rather than operate as it had, with each division having its own performance management program.

The present performance management system is based, as with Case Corporation, on competencies identified as key to Sonoco's success. Sonoco uses four competencies for all employees and then adds additional competencies for those in executive or leadership positions. All employees are assessed on business and technical knowledge, communications, customer satisfaction, and teamwork and collaboration. In addition, leaders at Sonoco are evaluated on three other competencies:

visionary leadership (including accountability), coaching, and innovation and risk taking. Corporate executives have one other competency: practice of diversity management.

Employees have information available that makes clear why all these competencies are important, the positive behavior related to these competencies, and examples of poor behavior. As far as objectives are concerned, the company uses a cascading process that links corporate goals to division goals to department goals and down to individual employees.

The process begins with a formal performance planning meeting based on the key goals laid out in Sonoco's business plan. There individual performance objectives are set. Employees and their supervisors discuss employee competencies and outline a development plan for the year that will address shortcomings. As it should, the meeting includes discussion of the previous year's performance and developmental issues it raises.

Financial rewards for the previous year are discussed in the second quarter of the year when compensation changes are made.

In mid-year, business objectives and employee performance are reviewed. Whereas most organizations expect such meetings to be initiated by the supervisor, at Sonoco responsibility lies with employees. Indeed, throughout the process much of the responsibility rests with subordinates. So much so, that at the end of the year, employees complete a self-assessment and initiate a formal meeting with their supervisors. Together they discuss employee accomplishments, and the manager signs the form. Areas that require development are identified and noted for further discussion at next year's performance planning meeting. This end-of-year meeting should offer no surprises if manager and employee have been open and honest throughout the performance cycle. No numerical rating is given. Rather, feedback is provided in narrative to indicate employee strengths, weaknesses, individual objectives, and the skill training plan for the coming year.

How has Sonoco changed its performance management system?

First and foremost, performance management is a forward-looking process, with much attention focused on employee development rather than simply giving each and every employee a rating. It is also very much a process rather than a single event.

The competency-based system helps employees understand the importance of their goals and the relationship to Sonoco's values and direction.

Responsibility isn't the manager's. Rather, it rests where it might more appropriately belong – in the hands of employees. Certainly, Sonoco's system encourages buy-in by the employees because they are active participants in the setting of goals and meetings. Many employees also have a voice in the areas they consider critical for development.

Perhaps most important, the 360-degree feedback system is built around the competency model and both are integrated with the performance management system. This arrangement erases doubts about the worth of goals set or importance of values considered.

THE LINK BETWEEN RECRUITMENT/RETENTION AND PERFORMANCE MANAGEMENT/REWARDS

Companies that aim to attract talented employees and keep these high performers often find that they need to devote time and attention to revising their performance management and reward systems. Let's look at some corporate examples.

AlliedSignal

To attract and retain top talent, AlliedSignal tried variable pay programs but they proved not to be the answer – people regarded gain sharing as an entitlement and lost sight of its connection to higher performance. So the company turned to broader changes, including a cafeteria-style approach to benefits, and more options in its 401(k) program. These better responded to employee needs, but further research by AlliedSignal determined that greater employee commitment would come from a better worker-supervisor relationship. To ensure that employees felt their contribution was more valued, the company undertook supervisory training to ensure that supervisors had the communication skills to be clear, open, and honest with employees, that supervisors were willing to hear out employees' ideas, and that they were flexible enough to implement programs that weren't theirs – that were their employees'. The company decreed that employees complete 40 hours of learning annually, but further, that supervisors be actively involved in developing each worker's learning plan. Further, supervisors were taught how to provide recognition, including the worth of praise and need to acknowledge good work. And, needless to say, supervisors undertook coaching and counseling skill training.

AlliedSignal's goal wasn't only to increase job performance but also job satisfaction to encourage employees to remain. Although this initiative was prompted during the boom times when it was hard to acquire top talent, the skills that were taught are perhaps more beneficial in today's tough times when high performance is critical – which is what the supervisory training generates. One of AlliedSignal's core values is continuous improvement in employee performance.

Johnson & Johnson

J&J's employees are measured against standards that the company has developed focused on five key competencies: customer/marketplace focus, innovation, the ability to succeed in a highly complex environment, interdependent or partnering, and people and organization excellence. These standards have been compared to the spokes of a pinwheel wrapped around business results. To prosper professionally at J&J, an individual has to produce business results within the value system.

One of J&J's divisions is Ethicon Endo-Surgery, Inc., which offers a variety of recognition/rewards for performance. Management has found that no single reward-and-recognition effort is appropriate for all situations. So IMPACT is a very informal program that provides on-the-spot, immediate recognition when someone does something special, the J&J Achievement Award that any supervisor can recommend an individual employee or team for when they have done an extraordinary job, above and beyond their regular work, or come up with an innovation that gives the company tangible rewards; and the President's Quality Award, in place at Ethicon Endo since 1997, which is given to teams that have come up with innovations that have improved a process anywhere in the company.

Marriott

Formal performance evaluations are done annually. However, associates (aka employees) receive feedback on an ongoing basis during the year.

Currently many managers participate in a 360-degree assessment done six months into the process. Because of the ongoing feedback and 360-degree assessments, there are no surprises at the end of the year.

TRW

TRW believes firmly that rewards must be tied to performance. It is critical not only for high performance but also for attracting and keeping talented workers. So TRW has a Success Share Program under which bonuses are awarded based on how well the company and the specific group do each year. It also rewards individual performance, however. Individual performance appraisals are not regarded as a formality. They *must* be carried out on schedule, and each employee's annual increase is tied to how well he or she met the goals set at the previous year's appraisal.

The company has also extended stock options to a limited number of highly talented workers. The number of options each group receives is determined at the corporate level but the decision as to which individuals will receive them is made locally, by the managers best qualified to judge workers' performance.

Xerox Corporation

Xerox follows a model called "Managing for Results," similar to a Management by Objectives approach, that begins at the very top of the organization where objectives are set for the corporation. These objectives cascade down through the organization, all the way to its front-line employees. As yearly objectives are set throughout the organization, they are tied to very specific measurements. Employee retention is one goal; another is continuous improvement. Progress toward each and every goal is measured and rewarded.

REWARDS AND CORPORATE STRATEGIES

Reward and recognition programs aren't tied solely to employee satisfaction for purposes of recruitment and retention. Stock options don't carry much weight in today's high-tech IPOs, but during the boom years firms like Amazon.com were able to draw enthusiastic high performers to the startup, where employees worked long hours for salaries below market value. Southwest Airlines may be unionized but there are limited variable pay programs, perhaps the most inclusive is a corporation-wide profit-sharing program that encourages everyone to keep costs as low as possible. Everyone shares equally based on earnings and the company's profits. Those who work longer hours or fly extra trips receive a larger piece of the profit-sharing payouts. Initially the program paid a mix of cash and deferrals to retirement accounts, but employees chose in 1990 to make the total contribution on a deferral basis. In addition, employees can purchase stock with payroll deductions at a discount through the employee stock purchase plan.

The company sees the program as supportive of its entrepreneurial spirit as well as giving all employees a sense of ownership in the business.

Some companies have designed their reward program to sustain a customer focus, others to encourage the workforce to think like a team, still others to support a business turnaround, and finally to encourage support to a change in strategy.

Key Concepts and Thinkers

This chapter contains a glossary of terms and concepts tied to performance management and reward systems, like:

» behaviorally anchored rating scales;
» competency modeling; and
» 360-degree feedback.

From A to Z, here's a glossary to make you familiar with the terminology of performance and reward management.

Action plan – In the context of performance management, this is often the result of an agreement by manager and employee when the employee's performance fails to meet set standards, objectives, or results.

Annual assessments – Performance appraisals are conducted on an annual basis, with periodic reviews over the course of 12 months (either every three or four months).

Appraisal – A systematic way of assessing the performance of employees. Typically, appraisals consist of an annual interview with a senior manager. At the interview, targets are set against which future performance can be measured.

Base pay – The salary for job performance based on the importance of the position to the organization, labor marketplace, and other factors.

Behavior – What people do, the actions they take, the things they say. Behavior is what produces results, and it is one approach to measurement for performance management purposes.

Behaviorally anchored rating scales (BARS) – A means of assessment, scales are developed that reflect various aspects of employees' work. For instance, "group facilitation" might have "encourages quiet members to participate" as the behavioral anchor for the 4 on the rating scale and "imposes own thoughts on the group" as a 1 on the scale.

Bonus plans – Given as recognition of successful performance, bonuses are not as highly regarded today as once before, for fear that employees may come to expect them and view them over time as fixed pay.

Coaching – Ongoing feedback to help good and outstanding employees sustain performance and average performers improve their work. Often confused with counseling, the focus of which is solely on marginal performers, and mentoring, which is more often career-focused.

Competency modeling – The analysis of jobs to identify skills, ability, knowledge, and attitudes required to do the work. Models are developed from research, with critical incident interviews, focus groups, and structured surveys with those who do the work; strategy which ties the attributes that will be needed to contribute to the organization's future success; and values considered important to the company by its management.

Continuous learning – Development of employee skills, knowledge, and experience essential in today's rapidly changing workplace. In order for an organization to remain competitive, employees need up-to-the-minute information and the ability to use new technologies, adapt to organizational change, work in flatter organizations in which cross-functional skills and knowledge are required, and work effectively in teams and other collaborative situations.

Counseling – Coaching of troubled or troublesome employees with the purpose of improving the individuals' performance. A process, counseling involves creation of an action plan for job improvement. Failure of the employee to turn around performance can lead to termination.

Critical incidents – The manager documents significant work activities or events (both positive or negative) and places them in the employee's file. At the time of the formal appraisal, the manager uses these events to form a composite profile of the employee's performance.

Critical incident reports – Documentation based on observable behavior. Also referred to as performance journals, this paperwork is used to justify assessment decisions (e.g. pay, promotion, termination).

Developmental goals – Besides work-related goals, experts advocate that managers set developmental goals with employees designed to close gaps in performance from the previous year. Employee development is recommended to be part of the annual assessment.

Developmental needs – A gap between how a person is currently performing and how the person needs to perform.

Documentation – Records of performance maintained on each and every employee to be used to verify conclusions reached in the appraisal process.

Evaluation criteria – The standards to be used to measure an employee's job performance.

Expatriate – A manager or skilled worker who is a foreigner in the country where he or she is working and living. Expatriates sent to live in unappealing places expect to get a number of generous perks (see "Fringe benefits" below) to compensate. In general, the less pleasant the destination, the more perks the employee gets. A case in point: it can cost three times as much to send a person to Moscow as it does to send him or her to Paris.

Extrinsic rewards – Rewards provided by the organization, by the manager, or by others in recognition of the job done. Different from intrinsic rewards that come from within an individual due to good feelings people get from the work itself, enjoyment with confronting and overcoming challenges, satisfaction in helping others or accomplishing something worthwhile, or simple pride in doing a job well.

Feedback – Information, provided to a person, which addresses the prior behavior of the person or the results of that behavior. Feedback is usually intended either to reinforce behavior or to suggest changes. It can be formal, during the performance appraisal process or when a performance improvement agreement is required to correct poor performance, or informal, in response to positive or negative behavior observed by a superior.

Fringe benefits (aka benefits, perks) – Rewards given to employees in addition to normal wages or salaries, they include things like pensions, private health insurance, expense accounts, low interest loans, and (less obviously) pay for time not worked (during holidays or sickness). For many managers they can amount to more than 30% of salary, a reality often ignored. Fringe benefits can disguise the real value of an employee's remuneration.

Gain sharing – Benefit plans that share financial savings from increased productivity, cost savings, and quality improvements with those instrumental in achieving these results.

Glass ceiling – A phrase taken from the title of the book *Shattering the Glass Ceiling*, written by Marilyn Davidson and Gary Cooper,[1] referring to the invisible barriers that may prevent women from climbing to the top of the management ladder. In the European Union as a whole, for instance, women make up almost 40% of the workforce yet less than 2% of top managers are women.

Goal setting – The process by which employee and supervisor set objectives or results to be accomplished over the course of the year. A goal itself is a desired or required future outcome. At the end of a set period, the results actually achieved are compared to the original goal to determine success. Goals are the "what" side of the performance coin; competencies are the "how" side – the capabilities that need to be brought to bear in their pursuit.

Golden parachute – An expression coined in the 1980s to describe the employment contracts that top managers had to ensure that they received huge compensation on their dismissal for purposes other than for cause.

Incentive – Anything that encourages an employee to work harder and to be more productive.

Instrument – Any kind of device that is used to collect information in a structured, systematic way. Examples of instruments are tests, performance evaluation forms, and survey questionnaires.

Job analysis – Comparison of the tasks and activities, KSAs, and traits and characteristics of a job with other jobs that are inside and outside the organization. Used by HR, the process is used to consider, categorize, and assign salary grades to all of the jobs within the organization.

Job content – Reduces to words what people do in a particular work role. Job content is an inventory of what parts of the job are to be appraised and are the foundation for job descriptions and later performance appraisals.

KSAs – Reference to knowledge, skills, and abilities, the foundation for job content analysis and competency modeling.

Likert, Rensis – A psychologist who developed an influential concept of management styles while working for the Institute for Social Research at the University of Michigan. He classified managers as: authoritarian managers, who believe in coercing people to do as they are told; benevolent authoritarian managers, who use a carrot rather than a stick to get people to do as they are told; consultative managers, who talk things through with junior colleagues even though they make the decisions in the end; and participative managers, who encourage employees to make decisions together and then watch over them to ensure that they achieve their targets. The second style is the most common but the last is the most effective in the long term.

Management by Objectives (MBO) – As an appraisal tool, MBO enables manager and employee to set a group of specific goals together and measure and evaluate the employee's performance against it.

Mileposts – Checkpoints that can be set and used to ensure a goal is on track, often quarterly or trimester updates of job performance in which work done is compared to goals set.

Motivation – What moves people to behave in particular ways.

Narration – This approach to doing assessments has the manager developing an essay that answers the question, "How would I evaluate this person's performance over the past year?" The value of this technique is dependent on the observational, memory, and writing skills of the manager. The assessment technique is questionable since there are no set guidelines.

Norms – The informal behaviors that operate within a work group. Organizational surveys often try to detect what kinds of norms are in place and how strong they are. Action plans might then focus on how to strengthen or spread constructive norms or how to fix dysfunctional norms.

Peer evaluation – Measurement of an individual's performance is carried out by everyone in a group designated by the manager or human resources department.

Performance agreement – A written agreement between an employee and his or her supervisor that identifies goals to be achieved within a specific time period.

Performance appraisal – The process by which the performance of employees within the organization is measured. Made up of six steps, it involves:

1 development of objectives or goals or results by manager and employee working together;
2 ongoing feedback throughout a 12-month period based on written records kept of job behavior;
3 review of all pertinent documentation before end-of-year assessment;
4 select suitable location for meeting, one in which the parties will not be interrupted and employee will feel at ease;

5 appraisal meeting in which manager shares conclusions about the
employee's performance over the year;

6 creation of an employee development plan to address problems
over the past year or other decisions made related to the appraisal.

Profit sharing – A portion of the organization's profit shared with
each employee as a percentage of base pay, profit sharing is the
original organization-wide variable pay plan.

Questions – As part of the performance appraisal, the manager will ask
a variety of questions. Open-ended questions are those that cannot
be answered with a yes or no but require an opinion or expression
of feelings. Reflective questions repeat the statement that the other
person has made in the form of a question, thereby encouraging
clarification or expansion about what was said. Directive questions
are used to solicit information about a particular point or issue,
usually reserved until after the other person has finished talking
on the subject. All three forms of questions are useful in drawing
the employee into a thorough discussion of job performance and
personal development.

Results-oriented appraisals – Similar to the MBO approach, the
results-oriented approach ties goals to specific corporate strategies
or tactics. Another term is output.

Salary scale – A table that shows the salaries paid to employees at
different levels (grades) in an organization. The scale may define
salaries with a particular grade according to rank, length of service,
special skills, and time spent in the grade.

Self-appraisals – Employees evaluate their own performance, typically against objectives they and the manager have set.

Skill-based pay – Pay is determined by the skills of the employee
rather than the job to which the employee is assigned. The basis
of skill-based pay (or "pay for knowledge") is paying more as
employees demonstrate that they are obtaining and using more and
more skills that are valuable to the organization. Most skill-based pay
organizations are organized into work teams or self-managing work
groups.

SMART goals – SMART refers to five characteristics of goals: specific,
measurable, action-oriented, realistic, and time- and resource-con-
strained. Good performance goals adhere to all five requirements.

Standards – The level of performance by which employees' work is measured. Minimal performance is set and the standards reflect these.

Stock options – A type of variable pay, stock options plans offer employees the chance to purchase their for-profit company's common stock at some time in the future at a specific price. Traditionally stock options were reserved for executives and senior managers because options were believed to offer stakeholder status to employees in a position to have a meaningful impact on organization performance. During the e-commerce boom, employees were given options to accept low base pay. The dot-com shakeout diminished the worth of such compensation.

Succession planning – The process and actions that aim at identifying and developing a pool of potential successors for senior or key jobs in the future. Unlike replacement planning, succession planning is more strategic, proactive, long term oriented, and development-focused.

Theory X – One extreme of a spectrum of views about humans' attitudes to work. Theory X and Theory Y were expounded by Douglas McGregor, a social psychologist who was professor of management at MIT for a decade from the mid-1950s. Theory X is the traditional view of things: humans have a natural dislike to work and will avoid it if they can. Therefore, they have to be coerced and threatened to get them to do their work. Experience has shown that managers who take this view generally get a hostile reaction from employees, which reinforces their original view.

Theory Y – This is the other side of McGregor's Theory X. It proposes that humans naturally find work satisfying, and that management systems built on that assumption will give individuals responsibility and freedom to attain the corporation's objectives under their own steam. Opponents of Theory Y say that the theory makes the assumption that all workers are self-motivated, which is not so.

360-degree assessments – This approach to assessments rates the importance of the skills and behaviors in a job and how successfully the job holder practices them. Employees rate themselves and are rated not only by their immediate supervisors but by peers, subordinates, other managers, even customers. That's the full circle of acquaintances, consequently the name "360."

Trait ratings – In this appraisal approach, employees are rated based on characteristics like good interpersonal skills, creativity, dedication, or teamwork. Courts look askance at trait rating since the traits rated are often broadly defined as the criteria for rating the level of performance associated with the trait.

Value statements – Strategic issues of importance to the organization that can be translated into behaviors and ultimately be the basis of performance assessments.

Weight – Used to signify that some competencies and goals are more important than others. Assessment tools place weights on importance and difficulty of tasks within jobs.

Wrongful dismissal (aka wrongful discharge) – Firing an employee for a reason that is not sufficient to justify such action. In the US the law protects employees against what was once common practice. If wrongful dismissal can be proved in the courts, the victim has a right to compensation.

NOTE

1 Davidson, M. & Cooper, G. (1992) *Shattering the Glass Ceiling*. Paul Chapman Publishers, London.

Resources

Find out in this chapter about:

» articles;
» books;
» organizations; and
» Websites.

Here are articles, books, organizations, and Websites to help you successfully practice performance and reward management.

ARTICLES

» Cross, K. (2001) "The Weakest Links." *Business 3.0*, June

More companies are regularly firing their lowest-performing employees. While some companies try to revitalize the dead wood, others are finding it more efficient to simply "upgrade the team," the term Siebel Systems' CFO, Ken Goldman, gives for layoffs tied to job performance assessments. Siebel requires managers to turn over 5% of their poorest performers about every six months. This kind of bell-curve tactic may seem good for management, but it has prompted game playing from employees, like employees deliberately choosing to work in less-challenging groups where they can look good, and even nurturing managers who argue that they don't have any poor performers left after the first cut has been made.

» Ferracone, R. & Borneman, J. "Time to Rethink Compensation." *HR.com* (hr.com/index.cfm/WeeklyMag/94A84C60–59C2-llD5–9AC6009027E024)

As long as the market is going up, options work well – shareholders do well, executives feel well compensated for their efforts. But in a declining market, shareholders suffer and executives do not see the options as incentives. What should companies do? Rather than opt for a short-term fix, the author suggests companies step back and re-evaluate their entire long-term incentive program and make lasting changes that will address fundamental pay for performance and retention issues. Questions to raise: What are the goals of our long-term incentive plan? Do we need to focus on long-term internal (operational) as well as external (stock market) performance? To what extent should absolute measures be balanced against relative measures of success? Should we consider using other vehicles in addition to stock options, including "career shares" or ownership programs?

» Guinn, K. (1987) "Performance Management: Not Just an Annual Appraisal." *Training*, August

The author describes the differences between performance appraisal and performance management – how appraisals are part of a process that includes coaching and counseling and establishment of standards or goals against which performance is measured.

» Laabs, J.K. "Demand Performance for Benefits." *Workforce.com* (workforce.com/archive/article/000/6369.xci)

The author contends that employees should look at benefits as part of their total compensation package and consequently treated like the rest of the package – that is, tied to performance. The author notes a survey in 1999 by the American Compensation Association and Segal Co., a New York City-based HR consulting firm, that showed how some employers are using non-monetary compensation – particularly work/life programs – as part of their total rewards management strategy. The work/life programs currently used to reward employee performance are geared toward rewarding high performers with additional time to conduct personal business (e.g., flexible work schedules and paid time off).

» Prencipe, L.W. (2001) "Re-energize the Disengaged Worker." *Info-World*, April 9

Remember the old saw about the employee who retired but forgot to tell the company? The author believes that such disengagement is more likely to happen during periods of layoffs or mergers and acquisitions, in which a company's status is in flux, and her article prescribes a way to remotivate disengaged or burnt-out employees. Before coaching can begin, the author points out that such individuals need to be identified. Among the clues: the employee no longer is an active participant at meetings; whereas the individual once would pitch in during emergencies, he or she now sits on the sidelines; the employee develops the habit of long lunches or takes more sick time. While not all disengaged employees are worth bringing back into the fold – perhaps this individual was a marginal performer beforehand – action needs to be taken since one disengaged worker can affect the morale of the entire team.

» Williams, V.L. & Grimaldi, S.E. "A Quick Breakdown of Strategic Pay." *Workforce*. (workforce.com/archive/article/000/58/82.xci)

The authors observe how an effective total compensation system is made up of both cash and non-cash rewards – all designed to support the company's compensation philosophy, motivate and reward performance aligned with critical business objectives, and attract and keep top talent. The philosophy of strategic pay involves identification of desired market position by articulating where the company wants to position pay levels with respect to competitive market practice. Once that philosophy is established, the company needs to give consideration to the issues of base pay, including merit increases; performance-based variable pay; long-term incentive compensation; and non-cash rewards and recognition.

» Whitcombe, J. (2001) "Can Pay for Performance Really Work?" *Workforce*, August.

While pay for performance can be a solution for some organizations in search of new concepts, it's not the answer for every one. The range of options about pay for performance is broad and deep. Its proponents say that rigorous, long-term pay for performance systems offer effective methods for helping companies continually improve the workforce while getting and keeping the best people. Opponents argue that incentive pay plans tend to pit employees against one another, erode trust and teamwork, and create what critics call dressed-up sweatshops. The author identifies shortcomings in performance pay plans and offers case studies to demonstrate how it can be made to work.

» Zingheim, P.K. & Schuster, J.R. "Merit Pay Usually Fails – Can You Fix Yours?" (www.hr.com)

Merit pay has received a bad name. HR and compensation managers question its worth, saying things like: "It doesn't really pay for performance." "All it does is to call a 'cost of living' increase pay for performance." "It's just an entitlement with a different name." In this article, the authors suggest how to make "merit pay" a real "merit pay" solution. Among the advice: decide what you're paying for; give enough money for "merit;" develop measures for merit pay; put money where performance is expected; use variable pay for performance; dump internal equity from pay concerns.

» Zingheim, P.K. & Schuster, J.R. "Value Is the Goal." Workforce.com (www.workforce.com/archive/article/001/12/97.xci)

Variable pay should stimulate performance so long as it is properly used. Variable pay needs to be re-earned year after year, but too often it is treated as an entitlement, something that everyone receives each year. After stating their main premise, the authors describe a variety of variable pay plans, from goal sharing, in which short-term variable pay is given for meeting goals aligned with the operating plan, to win sharing, in which rewards are given based on increased financial performance, to profit sharing after a specified level of return has been achieved, to team variable pay.

BOOKS

» Bacal, R. (1999) *Performance Management*. McGraw-Hill, New York.

Yes, this is a hands-on book that describes how to get top performance from employees, but it also describes various performance management systems and offers guidelines on how to make best selection of the system for your organization. Contains many short chapters that provide several examples of how to apply performance management concepts in the workplace.

» Berger, L.A. & Berger, D.R. (eds) (2000) *The Compensation Handbook: A State of the Art Guide to Compensation Strategy and Design*. McGraw-Hill, New York.

Experts in compensation have been assembled to contribute to this huge edition called "the bible of compensation." Within its pages there is up-to-date help with base compensation, variable compensation, executive compensation, performance and compensation, compensation and corporate culture, and international compensation. Particularly relevant to this book is a full section on performance and compensation, with discussion of best practices.

» Bowen, R.B. (2000) *Recognizing and Rewarding Employees*. McGraw-Hill, New York.

This book looks at the new workforce and suggests rewards and recognition that are most appropriate. The author talks about the differences between bribes and undue flattery, and pay for performance and meaningful praise, and how to balance intrinsic and extrinsic rewards.

» Cadwell, C.M. (1994) *The Human Touch Performance Appraisal*. American Media Incorporated, Des Moines.

This book focuses on the process of conducting performance appraisals, not the paperwork or "forms to fill." The process described helps managers build on their employees' strengths so they can reach their true potential.

» Carter, L., Giber, D. & Goldsmith, M. (2001) *Best Practices in Organization Development and Change*. Jossey-Bass/Pfeiffer, San Francisco.

This book describes how 17 global organizations apply OD/HRD to five critical issues: organization development and change, leadership development, recruitment and retention, performance management, and coaching and mentoring.

» Coens, T. & Jenkins, M. (2000) *Abolishing Performance Appraisals: Why They Backfire and What to Do Instead*. Berrett Kohler, San Francisco.

Many organizations are beginning to question deeply whether appraisals are necessary and consistent with today's work culture. This book looks at the flaws of appraisal programs – like the excessive paperwork it demands – and identifies not only cures for these problems but goes so far as to propose the elimination of appraisals and creation of alternative methods of monitoring performance.

» de Board, R. (1994) *Counselling Skills*. Gower Publishing, Aldershot.

Done correctly, counseling can open up communication between boss and employee and lay the groundwork for improvement in employee performance. Counseling is very much a managerial responsibility and this book is designed to teach managers what they need to know to put an end to sub-par performance and, if necessary, make the tough termination decision that failure to improve demands.

» Fisher, S.G. (1997) *The Manager's Pocket Guide to Performance Management*. HRD Press, Amherst, MA.

This booklet provides guidelines for managers to help their employees perform to potential. Topics include analyzing performance, identifying performance gaps, developing strategies to maximize performance, and recognizing and rewarding performance.

» Fraser, J.A. (2001) *White-Collar Sweatshop: The Deterioration of Work and Its Rewards in Corporate America*. W.W. Norton & Company, New York.

Life at work for many has become a corporate nightmare, with seven-day-a-week workloads, reduced salaries and benefits, virtual enslavement to technology, and a pervasive fear about job security. With facts, figures, and telling case histories, the author chronicles the growing trend of shrinking paychecks and disappearing benefits and other squeezes that make it tougher to get top performance from even the best of your employees.

» Grote, D. (1996) *The Complete Guide to Performance Appraisals*. AMACOM, New York.

An in-depth description of developing performance appraisals as part of an overall performance system, with specific chapters on how to create a performance appraisal system and how to make it work.

» Kohn, A. (1999) *Punished by Rewards: The Trouble with Gold Stars, Incentive Plans, As, Praise, and Other Bribes*. Houghton Mifflin, New York.

Drawing from hundreds of studies, Kohn demonstrates that people actually do inferior work when they are enticed with money or other incentives. The more we use artificial inducements to motivate people, the more they lose interest in what we're bribing them to do.

» Moglia, T. (1997) *Partners in Performance: Successful Performance Management*. Crisp Publications, Menlo Park.

The author explains the importance of people working together to set performance guidelines and a model or process to evaluate those guidelines. The author also explains the importance of gaining employee commitment to the process.

» Nelson, B. (1994) *1001 Ways to Reward Employees*. Workman, New York.

This best-seller is a guide to rewards for every conceivable situation. From the spontaneous gesture of praise to formal company-wide payment plans, it contains hundreds of ways to say thank you to top performers.

» Plachy, R.J. & Plachy, S.J. (1993) *Results-Oriented Job Descriptions*. AMACOM, New York.

The authors recommend focusing on results when writing job descriptions, to change their emphasis and enhance their usefulness. They provide more than 225 models that can be used or adapted to create job descriptions.

» Putzier, J. (2001) *Get Weird! 101 Innovative Ways to Make Your Company a Great Place to Work*. AMACOM, New York.

Among the ideas offered by the author are ways to bring out the very best performance from your employees and to reward your workers when they perform to their full potential.

» Risher, H. (ed.) (1999) *Aligning Pay and Results: Compensation Strategies That Work from the Boardroom to the Shop Floor*. AMACOM, New York.

This book answers numerous questions of HR managers related to reward management, such as: Who decides performance goals? Are results quantified in purely financial terms? If not, how do you measure intangible results? How do you build "stretch" into goals without discouraging employees? How do you compensate members of a team who make differing levels of contribution to the end result?

» Saunders, R. (2000) *The Agile Manager's Guide to Performance Appraisals*. Velocity Press, Bristol, VT.

The book takes managers through the performance appraisal system, from setting useful objectives to documenting employee performance, to assessing marginal performers constructively, to holding fruitful appraisal meetings.

» Schuster, J.R., Zingheim, P.K. (1996) *The New Pay: Linking Employee and Organizational Performance*. Jossey-Bass, San Francisco.

The authors present a strategic, total compensation approach to the subject of rewards, suggesting how organizations can use base pay, variable pay, and indirect pay to accomplish key priorities.

» Schuster, J.R., Zingheim, P.K. (2000) *Pay People Right: Breakthrough Reward Strategies to Create Great Companies*. Jossey-Bass, San Francisco.

The authors build a business case for retooling reward systems, showing how companies can integrate reward systems fully with business strategy in order to pay people for the true value they add. The authors observe that pay is often one of the last considerations of management but it should be among the first if organizations want to create a win-win partnership between themselves and their staffs.

» Stone, F. (1999) *Coaching, Counseling & Mentoring*. AMACOM, New York.

This book proposes a three-tiered approach to performance management, differentiating coaching from counseling from mentoring. Readers learn how to practice each of the three with individuals and with teams.

» Weiss, A. (1994) *Managing for Peak Performance*. La Brisas Research Press, East Greenwich, RI.

The author focuses on the importance of understanding human behavior and its relationship to performance. He explains why this is essential for a manager responsible for motivating himself or herself and others to perform. The book includes self-evaluation tests to assess an individual's behavioral style.

» Wilson, T.B. (1995) *Innovative Reward Systems for the Changing Workplace*. McGraw-Hill, New York.

The author argues that most pay systems are tied to level or position, not top performance, collaboration, and teamwork. The last are behind his Reward Smart system. Job-based pay systems need to be replaced with ones that reinforce the special competencies and contributions of individuals and teams, creating team incentives, gain sharing, and project-oriented reward systems. Thirty-nine case studies reveal how each company devised its own blend of salary systems, incentives and bonus programs, personal recognition, and other rewards to recognize superior work and motivate high performance.

OTHER

» Society for Human Resource Management: www.shrm.org/hrmagazine/archive/

You don't have to be a member of SHRM to access the many articles available at this membership organization's home site. In particular, check out the sections of the site devoted to performance management and compensation and benefits.

» HR.com

Visit this free resource of articles on a variety of human resources issues, including performance management and compensation and benefits. Produced in Canada, the Website (www.hr.com) includes articles and white papers on a variety of people issues, accessible at no cost.

Ten Ways to Manage Performance and Rewards

This chapter will give you help on:

» using performance management to maximize your employees' contribution;
» using intrinsic rewards, as well as extrinsic rewards;
» effectively and efficiently applying your firm's appraisal process;
» counseling troubled employees; and
» using raises and other rewards as part of performance management.

There are ways that managers can manage work and pay to the benefit of their employees as well as their organizations. Managers may feel that they have little control over the financial and other recognition their employees receive, but that's far from the case. Managers can practice performance management in a way that maximizes the contribution of their employees, and then take advantage of extrinsic and intrinsic rewards to sustain the high performance.

In this chapter, we will look at 10 specific steps that managers can take to sustain the work of superstars, maintain the performance of good employees, and address the performance problems of poor performers, including making the tough decision about termination. In this chapter, we will look at how to:

» develop SMART goals;
» tie performance to rewards;
» counsel troubled employees;
» recognize good work; and
» use non-monetary rewards when dollars are limited.

1. UNDERSTAND YOUR COMPANY'S PERFORMANCE MANAGEMENT/REWARD SYSTEM

This means more than knowing which forms to fill out when. It's imperative that you appreciate the reasons behind each step in the process. Likewise, understand the rewards you can and can't provide. Employees may ask, and you want to be knowledgeable about those extrinsic rewards that are part of the performance management/reward management programs. You should also be alert to the non-monetary rewards within your power to offer.

I was recently told by an employee about her boss's refusal to grant her a personal half day. The administrative assistant had put in some extra hours of work without pay and needed the time off to deal with a problem related to her school-age daughter. The supervisor told her that it was against policy. Needless to say, the employee went to the human resources division. She learned that it was within her manager's power to grant the request. Did the manager grant the request? Ultimately yes, but even so, his failure to know that he had that right made him lose respect in the eyes of the employee.

Besides information, you need to be skilled in handling the various stages of the performance management process – from reaching agreement with employees on goals to providing coaching as needed, to offering constructive feedback (note I didn't say "constructive criticism" which is an oxymoron), to counseling in the event of sub-par performance.

2. SET GOALS OR OBJECTIVES

The first step in performance management is identification of goals or objectives. These objectives or goals may be in the form of standards of output or goals or results tied to organization-wide performance goals. These objectives should fall into the category of SMART goals; that is, they should be specific, measurable, attainable, realistic, and time-relevant. Only then can the manager monitor employees' performance against the goals.

This might sound a lot easier than it is. First and foremost, goals must be linked to organizational goals – either department objectives or organization-wide goals. But there may be many goals that fall into that category. And it is hard to avoid the temptation to take on those goals that are most interesting or fun to accomplish. Consequently, you need to work with the employee to be sure that you pick those goals with the greatest relevance. Certain goals will help your organization come closer to achieving its strategic objective than others. Ideally, you and your team need to concentrate your efforts on those few goals that have the biggest payoff.

"Few" is a key word here. Just as you can't do everything at once, so neither can your employees. A few goals are the most you should have your employee attempt to conquer at any one time.

And, of course, at milestones – those quarterly or trimester reviews – revisit the goals. Update them as necessary. The world of business today is anything but static, so periodically assessing the goals with the employee is important to make sure that they are still relevant to the bigger organization picture.

One additional bit of advice: Word the goals effectively. Begin with an action verb, describe the immediate results if necessary, include the date by which you want the goal achieved, and define the overall result desired (in terms of quality, quantity, increased sales or reduced costs, or some other factor).

I use the term "goals" here but different performance management systems use different terms. Some systems use "results" or efforts that are part of the employee's job that will contribute most to the employee's success and that offer the greatest benefits to the organization. Standards are performance goals, often the same for each employee in the same job. For instance, a standard for a customer service rep might be to process no fewer than 40 orders per week. A developmental goal is a skill, ability, or job knowledge that needs shoring up. Finally, "performance factor" relates to behaviors linked to corporate values. In the case of the last, they have to be translated beyond the behavior (e.g. show initiative) into specific SMART goals.

3. MONITOR BEHAVIOR

To some extent, I'm suggesting that you manage by walking about. Remember MBWA (Management By Wandering Around) as described by Peters and Waterman in *In Search of Excellence*?[1] This doesn't mean you hover over your employees. Certainly don't hover over the same employees each and every minute, even if they are problem performers. Sub-par performers only learn how to look busy when you are around, and your more productive workers get the wrong impression about you – they begin to think that you don't care about their performance.

When you visit with your employees, learn to spend the majority of the time listening, not talking. Yes, you want to share department goals with members of your team. In a long-ago radio program, a Canadian mountie, in talking about perspective, told a trapper, "The view only changes for the lead dog." MBWA gives you the chance to let employees know that direction has shifted and why so they won't trip over themselves. On the other hand, it is an equally great opportunity to ask questions and listen to the words and tone of employees as they respond. Watch, too, as they work to see how they do their jobs.

4. DON'T OVERLOOK YOUR PERIODIC REVIEWS

Don't let your busy work schedule keep you from the milestone meetings that are very much a part of most performance management systems. Even if they aren't part of your company's program, consider holding such sessions to review progress toward goals or adherence to standards, or whatever the terminology within your performance management system.

During the milestone meetings, you want to discuss and agree on the quality of the employee's performance to date, identify strengths and areas for improvement, create an employee development plan if improvement is needed, and agree on your expectations (what's to be done and how by the next quarterly review).

Each of these milestone meetings should be substantive. Set aside an hour or more with each employee. No matter how many meetings that adds up to, be sure that each is free of interruptions. If you work in a cubicle, hold the meeting where your conversation won't be overheard, like a conference room. If you have a private office, make sure you aren't interrupted.

Given the importance of these sessions, you shouldn't try to "wing" them. What does that mean? During each quarter, you should have been observing your employee and jotting down notes – yes, documenting what you see. Prior to your milestone meetings, you should read your notes and come prepared with specifics. Have a messy office like mine? Make an effort to move the papers off your desk so they don't distract you from the discussion or suggest to your employees that your mind is not totally on the meeting.

5. ASSESS MARGINAL EMPLOYEES CONSTRUCTIVELY

It isn't only goof-offs or those with poor attitudes who fail to meet the standards or achieve the key results or outcomes you have agreed upon. Among other reasons goals aren't met include:

» a lack of resources to make things happen;
» work that doesn't match the employee's abilities;
» training deficiencies; and
» employee carelessness.

The purpose of counseling is to identify the cause for a gap between expectations and performance and give the employee the chance to turn his or her performance around. So the first step is to identify the cause.

Since the employee may deny the existence of a problem, you may want to bring your notes that detail observed behavior with you. That will support your remarks. The records you keep should be based not on rumor or hearsay but rather incidents you have observed or carefully investigated after being told them by another employee, another manager, or a customer. Just document the facts. Whatever you may personally feel about the employee's behavior, it is not part of the record. The records you prepare must be such that a third party reading them will agree that the individual failed to do his or her job as expected. That's the purpose of the documentation.

For the counseling meeting, you may want to yellow highlight those incidents that support your concerns about the employee's job performance. The documentation should include the date, circumstances involved, and any others who were witnesses to the situation.

Ideally, based on the discussion, the marginal performer and you should reach agreement on the effort that the employee will make to turn his or her performance around. The discussion should be documented, with a copy provided for the employee and one placed in his or her personal records.

As part of the session, you will want to set up a timetable by which you expect to see an improvement in the employee's performance. At one time, managers could space such sessions a month or more apart. No more. The performance bar is raised. Employers expect an immediate improvement. Failure to see an improvement within a week or two may be sufficient to begin termination procedures in some organizations in some countries. Indeed, in some companies that practice employment-at-will, counseling sessions are unnecessary. An employer need do no more than notify an employee that he or she is no longer needed. If the company has notified its employees of such policy, there is no action an employee can take unless he or she can prove that the termination was discrimination-based.

Not only do policies differ by companies but by countries. As part of your training in use of the performance management/reward management systems, you need to determine both corporate and government regulations related to termination due to poor performance.

6. COMMUNICATE OPENLY, DIRECTLY, HONESTLY

If you are to encourage a behavioral change, you have to practice a five-step communication process as a part of your appraisal style.

First, describe any undesirable behavior. Don't waffle because you fear a confrontation with the employee or because you don't want to hurt the employee's feeling. Keep in mind that the longer you wait, the more difficult it may be to get the employee to change.

Next, listen to the response. You need to give the employee the opportunity to tell his or her side of the story or otherwise explain the behavior.

It's not enough to describe the problem. Next, you have to explain the implications. The employee needs to know the effect his or her behavior is having on workflow and on co-workers' performance. The employee also has to understand the consequences of continuing the behavior – for instance, being placed on warning, denied a raise, or fired.

In step four, you repeat your expectations. What kind of behavior or results do you want from the employee? If an employee is failing to achieve a key result or outcome, you want to examine his or her approach to see if you can identify a better way to accomplish the goal. This new way becomes the basis for a new key result or action plan.

The fifth and final step is to get a commitment for a change. You want to be sure that the employee understands your expectations and buys into the plan to achieve that. To encourage that, be sure the employee feels he or she had a voice in forming the plan.

Throughout this process, you will be listening but, as needed, you should also ask questions. Begin with open-ended questions that demand more than a "yes" or "no" reply. Follow up these with more pointed questions that probe for greater detail.

The point of this counseling session – indeed, each and every meeting with your employees – is to ensure that your employees recognize that they are accountable for their performance. Beyond that, you want your employees to recognize that you are there, and that they can come to you for help if need be. You want to create a supportive environment in which your employees will feel free to bring their questions to you to discuss openly and honestly.

7. CONDUCT THE ANNUAL APPRAISAL

Since you and your employees have been meeting on a regular basis to discuss progress toward achieving the goals, the conclusions at year-end should come as no surprise to either you or the employee. As you have done during the previous milestone meetings, you want to review the employee's performance and share with him or her your final evaluation for the 12-month period. That conclusion may be in a narrative form or be in the form of a rating. Whatever its format, it will influence the employee's position within the organization, which may prompt him or her to question your remarks or assessment, even refuse to sign any paperwork associated with the appraisal. If you feel the assessment is correct, then say so and provide evidence for your case. If the employee still refutes your assessment, let him or her do so in a memo attached to the appraisal when you submit it to the human resources department or put it in his or her personnel file. If the employee isn't satisfied, he or she may demand to go over your head. If so, let the employee. Write it down in your critical incident report that you have been maintaining about the employee.

If you identified problems during the year that additional training can address, bring that up during this assessment. Indeed, this can be a wonderful opportunity to prepare for the performance appraisal for the following year in that it will identify some development goals.

What about the raise that comes at the end of the year?

8. SPECIFY REWARD CRITERIA

Any merit rewards will be based on the quantity and quality of work. In setting goals, you should have specified the importance and difficulty in each goal, and that information will help to determine the rating or assessment in terms of merit increase. Each company has its own system. Let's assume that your company provides 5% raises to outstanding performers, 3% to average performers, and no raise for those who fail to meet the standards. The majority of your employees will receive a 3% raise. Those few who exceed your expectations will have earned the 5% raise. Those who failed to meet the results set should receive *nothing*.

What about variable pay? Variable pay is given for accomplishments beyond those specified in their jobs. Ideally, variable pay should be tied to one of the values advocated by the organization, like customer satisfaction, work quality, problem solving, work quantity, setting and achieving additional objectives, and improving work practices.

9. REWARD EVERYONE WHO MEETS THE CRITERIA

It's very easy to alienate employees by showing favoritism when it comes to the performance management/reward management. Consistency in both assessments and rewards are essential to ensure their ongoing support year after year. What if you are short of money? Look for non-monetary rewards and share those with all those who have earned them. If need be, give smaller rewards to all.

10. RECOGNIZE BEHAVIORS AS WELL AS OUTCOMES

There's nothing wrong with rewarding outcomes. If you've built all your goals around results, then it makes considerable sense. But if your organization skimps on recognizing desirable behavior, you are losing the opportunity to improve employees' work behavior and to motivate them to improve their work habits. And, most important, communicate to all the behaviors that your organization values. When it comes to rewards, keep in mind that the behavior you reward is likely to be repeated. Which represents both a warning and advice. Never reward someone whose behavior you would not want to have repeated. And you want to positively reinforce the kind of behavior you would like to see all your employees emulate.

NOTE

1 Peters, T.J. & Waterman, R.H. (1982) *In Search of Excellence: Lessons from America's Best-Run Companies*. Harper & Row, New York.

Frequently Asked Questions (FAQs)

Q1: How can we most effectively and efficiently recognize and reward employees?

A: That's the subject of this book on performance management and reward systems. See Chapter 1 for an introduction and an idea of the subject's relevance and importance.

Q2: What is the language of performance managers and compensation experts?

A: See Chapter 2 to find out.

Q3: How did the work of the behaviorists contribute to today's performance management and reward systems?

A: For answers, see Chapter 3.

Q4: How do you evaluate those who telecommute?

A: Advice can be found in Chapter 4.

Q5: What factors influence performance management and reward systems in global organizations?

A: See Chapter 5 for answers.

Q6: How are companies wringing the most out of their workforces?

A: To find out, see Chapter 6.

Q7: How are companies using rewards that drive high performance?

A: Read about success stories in Chapter 7.

Q8: What is base pay? How about variable pay?

A: Read Chapter 8.

Q9: Are you looking for a book or an article to increase your knowledge of performance management or rewards?

A: See Chapter 9.

Q10: How can you practice performance management to maximize the contribution of your employees? What about how you can use intrinsic rewards, as well as extrinsic rewards?

A: See answers in Chapter 10.

Index

Printed and bound in the UK by
CPI Antony Rowe, Eastbourne

Printed and bound by CPI Group (UK) Ltd, Croydon, CR0 4YY

13/04/2025

14656560-0001